God Uses Cracked Pots

Patsy Clairmont

PUBLISHING

Pomona, California

GOD USES CRACKED POTS

Copyright © 1991 by Focus on the Family

Library of Congress Cataloging-in-Publication Data

Clairmont, Patsy.
  God uses cracked pots / Patsy Clairmont.
    p.   cm.
  ISBN 1-56179-051-6 : $7.99
  1. Christian life—Anecdotes. 2. Christian life—1960- I. Title.
  BV4517.C55   1991
  248.4—dc20   91-16008
                                                                      CIP

Published by Focus on the Family Publishing, Pomona, California 91799.

Distributed in the U.S.A. and Canada by Word Books, Dallas, Texas.

Editor: Janet Kobobel

Designer: Timothy Jones

Cover illustrator: Greg MacNair

Printed in the United States of America

91 92 93 94 95 96 97 / 10 9 8 7 6 5 4 3 2 1

Contents

Acknowledgments

Thanks to all of you who supported this effort through your friendship and words of encouragement. I feel fortunate to have so many cheerleaders in my life.

I have often been aware of my mom's (Rebecca McEuen) prayers and am grateful for her love for Him and for me.

A big thank you to the Pauls for the loan of paradise during the countdown on my manuscript.

Thank you, Bob and Sarah, for helping to "prop" me up.

Mary-Lou, thanks for your willingness to put the manuscript into the computer. What a tedious task, which you did with such grace.

Ginny, your calls and notes of love and confidence were often the gentle nudge I needed.

I had tried to write previous to this book without success. I believe the key that unlocked my words was two-fold: the Lord's timing and my gifted editor, Janet Kobobel.

Janet, your expertise and wonderful gift of encouragement helped me to realize a lifetime dream. Thank you for being both firm and funny and knowing when to do which. Thank you for your editorial nurturing, for laughing at my stories and at times being my counselor as well as my friend.

For the past ten years, I have had the life- and ministry-expanding opportunity to work and travel with Florence Littauer on her C.L.A.S.S. staff. I would be amiss if I did not say a neon-sign thank-you to Florence for believing in me and for years of guidance.

Thanks also to Edith, Lana, Barbara, Jan, Loren, Betty, Nancy, Joyce, Will, Rose, Jo Ann and Carol for listening and laughing.

All We, Like Cracked Pots

Would you say you are a person given to bursts of babble? Do you just *love* to talk?

Imagine your family's reaction if you suddenly became a quiet person. Perhaps they would say, "Praise the Lord; He lives!" Because they know it would take the power of God to make that adjustment in your personality.

Likewise those of you who are quiet and sweet . . . oh, so *sweet*. If you were to speak up loud and clear, your family might say, "Praise the Lord; He lives, and so does she!" They have been waiting to hear from you.

Such changes are examples of God working in our cracked lives. Picture an empty pitcher with a network of cracks down the front. Now imagine that pitcher filled with light and a lid put on the top. Where does the light shine through? The cracks.

That is the same way the Lord's light shines through our lives. Not so much by what we do well naturally, but by what He must do in us supernaturally for it to be so. Like going from talkative to tranquil and from

1

cringing to courageous.

The stories in this book will validate that I am a cracked pot in need of divine repair. My prayer for myself is that His light shines through my cracks. And my prayer for you is that within these pages you will find reprieve from life's pressures, which add stress to your "pot," and that you might continue to shine brightly for Him.

Lookin' Good

I remember the day well. It was one of those times when everything goes right. I took a shower and fixed my hair. It went just the way I wanted it to, as it so seldom does. I pulled on my new pink sweater, giving me added color, since I need all the help I can get. I pulled on my gray slacks and my taupe heels.

I checked the mirror and thought, *Lookin' good!*

Since it was a cool Michigan day, I slipped on my gray trench coat with pink on the lapels. I was color-coded from head to toe.

When I arrived in downtown Brighton, where I intended to take care of some errands, I was surprised to find heavy traffic. Brighton is a small town, but it has a large health food store. Usually, I can park right in front and run in.

But today business was so brisk I had to park two blocks away. When your attitude is right, and it's a great day, however, inconveniences and interruptions are no big deal.

I thought, *I'll just bounce down the street in time to the sunshine.*

3

I got out of the car, bounced down the street, crossed the road and entered the store.

As I headed toward the back of the store, I caught my reflection in the glass doors of the refrigeration system. It reaffirmed I was lookin' good. While enjoying my mirrored self, I noticed something was following me. I turned and realized it was my panty hose!

I remembered the night before when I had done a little Wonder Woman act and taken panty hose and slacks off in one fell swoop. This morning I put on new panty hose and must have pushed the old hose through when I pulled on my slacks.

I believe they made their emergence as I bounced down the street in time to the sunshine. I remembered the truck driver who stopped his truck to let me cross. As I looked up, he was laughing, and I thought, *Oh, look! The whole world is happy today.*

So I waved. Little did I realize how much I was waving.

I assumed I had reached some amount of maturity by this time in my life, but I can honestly say that when I looked back and saw that . . . that . . . dangling participle, the thought that crossed my mind was *I am going to die!*

I knew they were my panty hose because the right foot was securely wrapped around my right ankle. I knew it was secure because I tried to shake the thing off and pretend I had picked it up in the street.

It's amazing to me that we gals buy these things in flat little packages, we wear them once, and they grow. Now I had a mammoth handful of panty hose and no place to pitch them. The shelves were crowded with groceries, and my purse was too small and full, so I stuffed them in my coat pocket. They became a protruding hump on my right hip.

I decided to never leave that store. I knew all the store owners in town, and I figured that by now they would have all their employees at the windows waiting for a return parade.

I glanced cautiously around the store and noticed it was Senior Citizens' Day. They were having their blood pressures read, so I got in line to avoid having to leave the store.

The bad news was no one noticed I didn't belong in line. The good news was I had an elevated blood pressure reading. Usually nurses take mine and say, "I'm sorry but you died two days ago." Today I registered well up the scale.

Finally I realized I'd have to leave. I slipped out the door, down the street, into my car and off for home.

All the way home I said, "I'll never tell anyone I did this, I'll never tell anyone I did this, I'LL NEVER TELL ANYONE I DID THIS!"

I made it home and got out of the car. My husband was in the yard raking.

I screamed, "Do you know what I did?!"

He was so proud to know his wife had gone through town dragging her underwear. I told him I thought we should move—to another state— in the night. He thought that was extreme and suggested instead that for a while I could walk ten feet behind him. After thinking that through, we decided it should be ten feet in front of him so he could check me out.

If you have ever done anything to embarrass yourself, you know that the more you try not to think about it, the more it comes to you in living color. As I walked through my house, the replay of what I did came to me again and again.

At last I cried out to the Lord, "You take ashes and create beauty, but can You do anything with panty hose?"

Almost immediately I realized that I had dragged a lot worse things through my life than panty hose. I dragged guilt, anger, fear and shame. I was reminded by the Lord that those were far more unattractive and distracting than my hose, for they prevented others from seeing His presence and His power in my life. I needed to resolve the pain in my past that I might live more fully today and look forward to my tomorrows.

Excuse me, but what is that you're dragging?

3

Guest Appearance

I had just finished doing a seminar with speaker Florence Littauer in Texas. She had made a special point of reminding the audience, "Be alert to the people the Lord places around you, especially on airplanes."

This was a new thought for me. When I get on an airplane, I have two people in mind—the pilot and me. I am in deep prayer for both of us.

As I headed for the airport, I reminded myself to be alert.

The first leg of my flight was uneventful. Then we changed planes in Chicago, and I noticed an airline attendant helping to board an older woman in a wheelchair.

When my row was called, I found I was seated in front of the older woman. We each had an empty seat next to us. A few minutes later a young couple came down the aisle. They stopped at the row of the older woman.

The young woman looked at her ticket, looked at the number on the overhead panel, then leaned into the woman and said with contempt,

"You're in my seat."

I turned around at this abruptness and saw the older lady shake her head and shrug her shoulders in an attempt to say, "I don't understand."

When the woman shrugged, the younger gal announced for all to hear, "You're in my seat!"

I tried to defuse the situation by saying, "Excuse me, but I don't think she speaks English."

The young woman turned on me and hissed, "I don't care what she speaks, I want her out of my seat." With that she called, "Stewardess."

Good, let the airlines handle her, I thought. I didn't want to deal with this traveling time bomb.

Usually flight personnel are trained to handle people problems. I think this attendant missed that class. She was almost as crude as the tactless traveler.

She looked down at the confused woman and demanded, "Let me see your tickets."

The older passenger realized this must be serious when she saw the attendant's uniform. Not understanding what they wanted, she gave her entire purse to the stewardess.

After rifling through her belongings, the flight gal found the ticket that verified the woman was in the wrong seat.

"Excuse me," I called to the attendant, "did you realize they boarded her in a wheelchair?"

"Really?" she whined, obviously annoyed. "This is going to make it harder to move her."

"Listen, why don't I move back there with her, and this . . . this . . . this couple can sit here," I said, pointing to my seat and the empty one beside me.

As I changed rows and took my new seat, I wanted this woman to know that all was well. I looked at her and smiled. She didn't respond.

Then I noticed she didn't have her seat belt on. I decided to help. It was a bigger job than I thought. I extended that belt as far as it would go, and it was prayer that closed it.

With that accomplished, I put on my belt, leaned back and closed my eyes. As the plane was taxiing for takeoff, I felt a hand on my hand. I turned and looked.

The older woman leaned over to me and slowly spoke the first words she had said, "You . . . first . . . Amer-i-can . . . be nice . . . to me."

Then taking her bracelet off her wrist, she pressed it into my hand and said, "I give you, you keep . . . okay?"

For a moment I couldn't respond. Then I swallowed the growing lump in my throat, slipped on the friendship bracelet and patted her hand. Her eyes filled with tears. My heart filled with gratitude.

Any room in your schedule for an unexpected guest?

Wiped Out

Mom, Mom, come quick! You've got to see what's on TV," Jason insisted.

Certain it would be something to make housework easier, I raced to the living room. Much to my surprise, the young girl on the screen leaned forward and announced, "I've got a zit right here," pointing to her nose. "But it's okay," she encouraged, "because I have a stick of Erase."

Confused (and unamused) I stared at Jason, who sheepishly confessed, "Well, I just thought maybe you could use it on those . . . those . . . wrinkles." He gestured toward my well-deserved grooves of maturity.

"These are not wrinkles," I stated clearly.

Jason surveyed my face again, as if he was reading a well-worn map. "They look just like wrin—" he stammered, losing confidence as I moved toward him.

"Jason," I interrupted, "this is depth! The good Lord has just entrusted some of us with more depth than others."

I marched off, feeling insulted or at least slightly defaced. I thought about the girl on TV and remembered her remedy. I began to picture a stick of Erase, in fact a great big stick. Then I mentally erased Jason.

That was such fun I began to think of others who had said or done something I didn't appreciate. I thought of our eldest son, Marty.

Each day I would meet him at the door with a melodic greeting as he returned from work. His typical response was to grunt. I erased him.

Then my husband came to mind. Now he never actually says it, but at times his attitude seems to shout, "Is this all you've done today?" Erase.

I was really getting into this game. I thought of other family members, neighbors, checkout clerks, co-workers, bank tellers, beauticians . . .

Now, the only drawback to this mental game was that everyone at one time or another had said or done something I didn't appreciate. By the time I erased them, it left me all alone. Somehow I didn't like the company.

I began to think of some things I've said or done I wished I could erase—like the last hasty word I felt "led" to say, or my unloving attitude with the clerk who was too slow, or the years I lost to agoraphobia, house-bound in fear. This game wasn't much fun after all.

Then I remembered that God provided a stick of Erase—a permanent eraser, the shed blood of Jesus. Our sins and iniquities He remembers no more—erase!

What a relief. What a release.

Pardon me, is that a stick of erase in your ha—

Hair-Raising

I can hardly believe that French braids are popular again. I was certain that type of braiding was leftover torture tactics from World War II and had worn out its welcome.

I certainly didn't welcome the times when Mom would call me into the living room where she had the weapons of warfare laid out before her: a brush and comb, a glass of water to help catch any stray ends, rubber bands and some ribbons. Sounds harmless enough . . . unless you're on the receiving end.

When Mom would plait my hair, it stayed in for a week. Those braids would not have dared move once she had placed them, nor did I while the braiding procedure was taking place.

I knew, from past experience, that the brush had a duo purpose of smoothing or rapping. She used quick staccato raps as reminders not to move. It worked.

The constant surprised look on my face in childhood pictures was actually caused by my coiffure. To implement this technique, Mom would first firmly grip three hanks of hair at the top of my head. It was imperative at this point to place one's knee in the middle of the braidee's back to secure one's hair hold, then pull until the victim's eyebrows arc and touch the first notch in the design of the braid. Come to think of it, I saw Hulk Hogan use that same tactic on one of his opponents . . . and win!

My mom always won, too. When she finished, my hair and I were enmeshed. Once Mom secured the lacing of hair and scalp with a rubber band, she then finished off the end with a ribbon, disguising this maiming updo with an innocent look.

People always commented on what a high forehead I had as a child. Actually that was my neck. It had been pulled up over my face in Mother's zeal to make the braids stay in. Had I continued to wear them that might not have mattered, but when the braids were finally released, my neck slid back down to my shoulders, leaving my face looking like a venetian blind.

The braiding did keep me from falling asleep in school. My lids were pulled so taut there wasn't enough skin left to cover my eyes.

Braids gave the boys a definite advantage, serving as handles to tug and jerk. Any girl with French braids would become hostile with the behind-the-back attack. Not only was it disconcerting, but we also knew if one of those braids was dislodged, our moms would redo the process.

Les and I have sons, but I've always wondered if we had had a daughter, would I have passed on this part of my heritage?

What painful part of your past are you passing on?

6

Forget It

I am the type of person who can walk from one room to another and not know why I've gone there. I know I had a reason when I began my trek, but I lost it on the way. Sometimes I try backing up in hopes it might come to me.

My family can usually tell this is the problem by the bewildered look on my face. Walking in reverse also seems to be a giveaway. Sometimes they try to help and other times they just let me wander aimlessly, figuring I'll wise up or wear out.

I try to blame this forgetfulness on age. But those who have known me for years remind me that my wires have never all been touching, although turning forty has seemed to loosen a few more.

I read in an article that after we turn forty, one thousand brain cells die each day. But according to the writer, it doesn't matter because we have millions . . . or was that billions, anyway lots of them. My problem is the cells I've been losing were filled with valuable information I meant to retain—like where I'm going, how old I am, the names of family

15

members, etc.

Names. Isn't it embarrassing when you know you know but you draw a blank? I realize that our names are important to us, and we don't want to be forgotten. That's why I think name tags should be mandatory. They should be pinned on us at birth and removed after the funeral. Think of all the awkward moments that could alleviate.

The guy, oh, what's his name, who sang "I Left My Heart in San Francisco" doesn't know how lucky he is. I left my bifocals in Indiana, my alarm clock in Ohio, my Bible on an airplane heading for Texas, my slip in Colorado, and heaven only knows where my watch is . . . probably with my sunglasses and keys.

Have you ever been digging through a drawer when all of a sudden you realize you don't know what you're looking for? If anyone is watching me, I just keep digging. I've found a lot of lost items that way.

It's disconcerting for me to dial the phone, and by the time the call connects, to find my mind has disconnected—I've forgotten whom I'm calling. Sometimes I hang up until I remember. Other times I listen in hopes I'll recognize the voice. Occasionally I've been brave and confessed to the anonymous party that I can't remember whom I dialed and hope they'll claim me.

The point I'm trying to make is . . . is . . .

Get the Kid

ommy, Mommy, Mommy, Mommy, Mommy, Mommy." Marty's persistence matched his rhythmic tugging on my blouse's hem.

I felt like screaming. In fact, I did.

To a little guy my response was probably similar to the release of Mt. St. Helens as I erupted, "What?!"

Why a mother waits so long to respond and allows the repetition to light her lava is beyond me. I only know that after spewing all over him I felt terrible . . . and so did he.

Where did all this volcanic anger come from? I seemed to always be upset at something or someone. Often my reactions were greater than the situation called for. I realized that Marty's little-child ways didn't deserve such strong responses.

Have you ever tried making things right when you know you're wrong but don't know how to admit it or quit it? That was often my frustration with Marty.

17

I'd send him to his room, leaving me with the realization that his punishment was greater than his crime. Then I'd try to make up by slipping him a Twinkie or playing a game with him. I soon found that Twinkies don't build good bridges of communication—too squishy.

During a prayer time, as I cried out to the Lord for help with my temper, especially with my son, an idea formed I believe was heaven-sent because it made a difference.

I was to pray with Marty before I administered any form of discipline. Sometimes those prayers sounded strange and strained as I almost shouted, "Dear Lord, help this miserable little boy and help his miserable mommy who wants so desperately to raise him in a way that would honor You."

By the time I said "amen," I was almost a reasonable person. I was able to see past my emotions and do what was in Marty's best interest.

Sometimes he needed a firm hand, but he was dealt with in love instead of anger, and the moment drew us together instead of tearing us apart. Many times all he needed was time and a mother's tender touch.

But one day that boy really ticked me off! I remember heading across the room for him like a high-speed locomotive, steam coming out all sides. I had one goal and intent—get the kid, get the kid, get the kid!

Just as I loomed over him, his eyes the size of saucers, he held up one hand and yelled, "Let's pray!"

Marty had learned a valuable lesson in life: "When Mommy talks to Jesus, we're all a lot better off."

Who lights your lava?

8

Half-Pint

My dad was a milkman when I was growing up, which might explain his nickname for me, "Half-Pint." His route was in the area where I attended school. I would sometimes see his truck from the window of my classroom as he delivered to his customers. One delivery stands out in my mind . . .

The girls' gym class was playing baseball on one end of the school field, and the boys were playing at the farthest opposite point. I guess that was supposed to help us stay focused on the game and not the guys. Actually, the boys were so far from us we didn't know they were there until . . . The Big Spill.

I was playing shortstop. I think I was given that spot because I was five feet tall (maybe that was why Dad called me Half-Pint).

I certainly wasn't put in the infield because I was good at catching the ball. Any hopes of that skill developing came to an abrupt halt when I stopped a line drive with my throat. That game forever drove home the term "hard ball." Ever since, when a baseball would head in my direction, I'd sidestep it or duck.

This particular day, my team was heading for our field positions after I had made the third out. I turned to face home plate when I spotted my dad's milk truck coming down a side road toward the field.

"Dad, Dad, hi Dad!" I shouted enthusiastically and repeatedly, while jumping up and down, waving my baseball mitt.

My dad spotted me and leaned out his truck's open door to return my greeting. His truck was the kind you drive standing up. As he waved, he veered too close to the edge of an incline, and the truck slid and tipped sideways. As the truck fell to the right, my dad jumped out the door to the left just as the load of milk shifted to the front. In those days most of the milk was in glass bottles, which we could hear shattering as the cases collided.

I couldn't move. I realized my dad was safe and unhurt, but there was still the ditched truck and damaged cargo. Tears began to run down my face. I felt responsible because I had distracted him.

As I stood staring at my dad while he surveyed his "milk shake," something else began to shake. It was the earth beneath my feet. I turned to see the boys' gym class stampeding across the field toward the girls' now halted game. They ran through and around us, out to the road, and over to my dad's dairy disaster. With the strength of young men motivated by the squeals of the girls, they were able to upright the milk "cart."

My dad was so relieved he didn't have to call a tow and the inside damage sounded worse than it was, he rewarded the boys by throwing boxes of ice cream bars into their midst.

The boys, equally thrilled with themselves, began to run down the road (now affectionately called the Milky Way) with their reward, laughing, with the rest of the group in hot pursuit. The poor coach was winded from blowing his whistle in attempts to regroup his "milk men."

I still had not moved. I was peeking through the webbing of my mitt. My gym suit was wet with tears.

Which just goes to prove . . .

It's not worth crying over spilled milk.

Kin

From my earliest years Aunt Pearl was my favorite kinfolk. Her Southern-country upbringing spiced her conversation with unexpected surprises that delighted the heart and often startled you into laughter.

Her wit was quick, but so was her temper. Even though she was my favorite, I knew better than to sass her. When I stayed at her house, which was every chance I could, you can bet your shoofly pie I obeyed her.

She was short and round and twirled her long brown hair into a tight little circle on the top of her head, capped by a hairnet. She moved fast, worked hard and relaxed fully. Aunt Pearl deeply loved the Lord, her family and a good meal, especially if it was served with laughter.

On one of her visits to Michigan, I remember her sitting at my kitchen table sharing life lessons with me.

She looked up and said, "Child, there ain't nothin' worse than a whuppin' from the Lord."

"A whuppin' from the Lord?" I puzzled.

"Yes, child, ain't you never had no whuppin'?" she questioned.

"I guess I have. My mom used to send me out to get a switch off the tree. The worst part of that whuppin' was picking the weapon to be used on you."

"That ain't nothin' like a whuppin' from the Lord," she insisted.

"I was at this here hospital a-waitin' in the hall to visit my friend," she continued, "when they come abringin' a woman down the hall on a gurney. The Spirit of the Lord said to me, 'Take that woman's hand.' "

She resisted, "Lord, I can't be a-takin' that woman's hand. I don't know her."

Again she heard Him state, "Take that woman's hand."

Aunt Pearl said at this point she began to "ar-gee" with the Lord, "afeard" someone "would be a-lockin' her up if she wusta be takin' that woman's hand."

The woman was rolled passed her, and for one moment their eyes met. Then she was gone down that long hall and through the double doors. Word came out a short time later that the woman had died.

With tears in her eyes, Aunt Pearl said, "Child, there ain't nothin' worse than a whuppin' from the Lord."

She believed the Lord had given her the opportunity to be the last person on this earth to touch that woman with His love, and she had failed to respond.

Then, with new determination in her voice, she announced, "Now when the Lord tells me to take someone's hand, I take her hand, her arm, I hug her neck, and I don't wanna let her go. 'Cause I don't want no more whoopin's from the Lord."

Have you been to the woodshed lately?

Leaning

Why, oh why did I ever say I would do this?

Fear was bobsledding through my body, creating havoc in my breathing apparatus and digestive tract. My tummy was gurgling so loud people were turning around, trying to decide who was guilty of such distracting sounds. When they looked in my direction, I'd roll my eyes toward the lady on my right, then I'd give a slight smile, as if we shared a secret about her noisy anatomy.

I was speaking for a ladies' retreat day to 250 women. I was only doing the book reviews, but I knew I was incompetent and would probably be incoherent by the time I crawled my way up on stage. I wasn't sure of my name much less what was in the six books I was to review.

I had notes, but they seemed so small now. My eyes didn't seem capable of focusing.

Maybe I needed a doctor. Yes, that's it . . . a doctor. I was way overdue for a physical. This seemed like a good time, so I stood to leave.

My friend Joyce had been observing my twitchy behavior and sensed I was bolting to run. She grabbed my arm, stuck a postcard in my face and said with authority, "Read this."

I wasn't in a reading mood, but something in her voice made me do it anyway. Still struggling with my eyes and concentration, the only thing I could make out was the title of what appeared to be a poem. It was called, "Lean Hard on Me."

The title was enough. I made an about-face and headed for the platform.

I kept repeating, "Lean hard on Him, lean hard on Him."

And I was. Had you been standing in the back watching me walk to the front, I'm sure I would have been at a thirty-degree angle I was leaning so hard.

I was now at the front row, and my friend Rose was announcing the book reviews. She introduced me as Klutzy Paramount. Well, the audience got almost hysterical over the slip.

Being inexperienced on stage, I didn't know what one should do when the audience was in gales of laughter at your name. I walked up the steps and started across the stage.

When they saw me they laughed harder. I'm not sure if they were agreeing the name fit my appearance or what.

As the hilarity began to subside, I leaned into the microphone and said, "My name is—" but before I could set the record straight, they were off in riotous laughter once again.

When they took a breath, I rattled off my reviews and retreated . . . relieved and rejoicing.

Are you leaving or leaning?

Main Attraction

I have a theory about why opposites attract. I think it's because we have a deep desire to get on each other's nerves.

My husband loves TV nature specials. I personally have never been that interested in the brain cells of a bumblebee or the anatomy of an anteater. He, in turn, does not understand my elation as I watch my video collection of "Winnie the Pooh" cartoons.

Les believes to be on time means to arrive a half hour early. I believe to enter as the big hand strikes the appointed hour is soon enough. Besides, if you arrive too early, you end up as part of the work crew.

Les loves his air conditioner . . . on high . . . while I have been accused of having a fixation for my electric blanket (which I wouldn't need so often if he'd turn off his air).

My husband longs to travel, but his job keeps him home. I enjoy being home, but my job keeps me on the road.

Country-and-western music is what Les sings along with, while I can lose myself in classical.

Les is your basic get-it-over-with shopper, while I'm a detailed investigative researcher.

I love books. Les looks forward to the newspaper.

My husband is a trivia buff. The only thing I retain is water.

He is a meat-and-potatoes man. I am a salad-and-veggie-plate gal.

Sometimes I think Les likes things just the opposite of me to agitate me, but then I remember . . . these are the things that drew me to him in the first place.

Do you let differences divide or define your relationships?

Hungry Heart

A s a child, my favorite pastime was a board game covered with colorful pictures of scrumptious sweets. Today, as an adult, I'm still following a tantalizing trail of tempting treats.

I've noticed that thin people don't have to work as hard as us hefties to make it down the trail. After all, we have to hold in our tummies. Tummy tucking (T.T.) takes stamina. I discovered a rich source of stamina can be found in French silk pie covered in mounds of shaved chocolate and also in goblets of tapioca smothered with dollops of fresh whipped cream.

Did you ever notice what happens to your anatomy when you hold in your tummy? First, T.T. punches your stomach into your diaphragm, which then catapults your esophagus into your tonsils. Your propelled tonsils, in turn, spiral your sinuses into your brain, causing you to blow your top!

If you release your tummy tuck position too quickly, because of the acceleration of gravity, you could bottom out. No wonder weight is such a heavy issue.

Speaking of heavy issues, try this appet-teaser test. It will help you weigh your eating choices. You might want to grab an eclair before beginning; tests can be strenuous.

Check appropriate boxes:

I eat because,
- ☐ I'm mad
- ☐ I'm glad
- ☐ I'm sad
- ☐ I've been bad
- ☐ I'm bored
- ☐ It's there
- ☐ Everyone else is eating
- ☐ I need it to sustain life

Depending on the results of your test, you, like me, may want to go on a diet . . . again.

I've learned from experience at times it is best not to diet. For instance, if you are on a business trip, vacation, expecting guests, eating out, holidays, stressful times, when you're moving, potlucks, picnics, in the evening or during daylight.

Sometimes I get miffed with a modified menu life-style. Tonight I rebelled and ate two pieces of homemade pumpkin pie and filled up— with regret. Usually I can bury my guilt, temporarily, under an avalanche of chocolate chip cookie crumbs. I have no room left this time, not even for Jell-O.

I wonder which weighs more: my groceries or my guilt? One makes my scale heavy, the other my heart.

Are you eating because you're hungry . . . or hurting?

13

Viewpoint

When your full stature measures five foot, you find yourself drawn to Scripture like "You shall say to this mountain, 'Move from here to there,' and it shall move" (Matt. 17:20, NAS).

I, believe it or not, was captain of a girls' basketball team in high school. I loved this position because I enjoy telling other people what to do.

But I had this problem, for me a mountainous problem, that I kept running into. Her name was Mount Kathy. She stood five feet eleven inches.

In those days, when giants walked the land, girls played half-court basketball. That meant you either shot the baskets or you guarded your opponents. I was a guard by choice. First, because I did not want to purposely embarrass myself attempting to get that big heavy ball into that exceedingly high hoop.

Second, I enjoyed being a guard and was pretty good at it. My height, or lack thereof, was at times to my advantage since I could move quickly around the half court. I was aggressive and as aggravating as a swarm of mosquitoes to the opposing forwards.

Then into my life lumbered Mount Kathy, who began to rob me of my reputation and my confidence. I just couldn't seem to get past her. I certainly couldn't go over her. The best I could do was get us into a jump ball situation.

Now that was a joke. I would jump my little heart out, and she didn't even have to move to her tiptoes. She'd stand flat-footed, looming over me, smiling down, braces and all, and then with a flick of her wrist direct the ball anywhere she wanted it to go. She certainly had no interference from me. Try as I might, I could not attain her altitude.

Probably just as well. I understand the higher you go, the harder it is to breathe.

I don't think Kathy read the same Bible verses I did, because no matter how often I said, "Move from here to there," she didn't budge.

Gratefully the basketball season ended, and now volleyball season was upon us. I once again was captain.

At our first game, after my serve I rotated to the front. I crouched, ready for serious play when I realized I was staring into a familiar pair of knee caps. Sure enough, it was Kathy.

I wonder if there are some mountains
He doesn't move . . . to keep us humble?

Musical Pews

I love to sing. I have yet to find anyone who loves to hear me. I don't sound that bad to myself, but I've had a number of people who have encouraged me in the art of humming.

I remember in junior high school my music teacher turned pale when she realized I had taken her class again. That semester she put me in the bass section with the boys. Her strategy worked; I was so embarrassed I switched to Home Ec.

Evidently voices don't improve with age. I remember singing a favorite of mine, "He Touched Me," at church one Sunday morning.

My friend Shirley was in the pew in front of me. I was really projecting on the chorus when she turned around, motioned me toward her, and whispered, "Trust me on this; He hasn't touched you yet, Patsy. Just mouth the words."

One good thing about a person's bathtub, there's no pew in front of you. Besides, I enjoy the acoustical benefit of the tiles when I shower.

I was into the bouncing chorus of "Zippity Doodah," as I lathered up, when my husband's panicked voice yelled through the door, "What's the matter?"

"Nothing, I was just singing," I called out melodically.

"Singing?" he asked incredulously. "I thought you were in pain!"

Even the shower isn't sacred anymore.

Invariably when I speak for a retreat, they seat me beside the soloist. That used to make me uncomfortable.

Sometimes I try what Shirley suggested: I mouth the words and hope people nearby think the singer's voice is coming out of me.

Why is it that those of us who can't sing marry those who can? Punishment maybe, for some past crime we forgot to confess.

Les has a delightful voice and knows a thousand songs. Except, I notice when I try to join him, he changes the words.

I've asked to join the church choir several times; but our director, Bill, always walks away laughing.

"That's a good one, Patsy," he says. "That's a good one."

Do the people around you seem uncomfortable with your singing? Take my advice—change pews.

Imprints

Isn't it funny what we remember about people?

In elementary school, my friend Diane had us call her Fred. Her hero was Fred Mertz of "I Love Lucy," and she wanted to grow up to be just like him.

I thought this was an unusual goal.

She called me Fatsy instead of Patsy.

Diane made us laugh a lot.

When I was in high school, a girl named Eva was in my gym class. She was the only girl I knew who shaved off her eyebrows and drew in new ones—very artistic, long, curved, full brows that were coal black.

When we had swimming class, her carefully applied artwork would wash away. I had never seen naked eyebrows before. I was fascinated. I tried not to stare, but sometimes I just couldn't help it.

Another unique feature about Eva was her honesty. When she found out I had a private scoop on a mutual friend, she said, "Well, whatever you do, don't tell me! I can't keep a secret."

I had never heard anyone admit that aloud, especially before she even heard the tantalizing tidbit. Eva impressed me with her bare brows and her heroic honesty.

I was from a good-sized high school, but when we got a new short-hand teacher, the school was abuzz. One reason was her unusual appearance. She must have been a trendsetter, because she was back-combing her hair long before anyone else. She had it so voluminous you could have hid a basketball in there, and no one would have known.

When I saw her I was certain I wouldn't like her. Who could like someone who looked like her hair had been inflated with a tire pump? She ended up being the best teacher I ever had.

For a while, as a young married couple, Les and I lived in a mobile home. Next door to us was a lot that was used for short-term travel trailers.

A couple in their thirties from Texas pulled into that spot on April 3, 1966. I remember the date because it was my twenty-first birthday. That was significant for two reasons: one, in that era it meant you had attained maturity; two, not one member in my family remembered this was my day!

To prove my grown-up status, I had been pouting all evening.

When I spotted our new neighbors backing into the lot, I invited them in for coffee in an attempt to cheer myself up.

The woman was unique-looking. She wore her hair in braids that were in a circle on the side of her head, and she had filled the circle with hibiscus. I hadn't seen anything like that since the movie *South Pacific*.

As we were getting acquainted, I mentioned it was my (sniff) birthday, and Les almost fell off the couch. He went from realization to repentance. He knew he had goofed.

Our guests, feeling the awkwardness of the situation, quickly departed. I felt they feared a family feud might follow, so they fled.

About an hour later there was a knock at our door. I opened it to find my new neighbor holding up a cake. She had gone home, baked, decorated and even swirled my name and all-important age in frosting on this creation.

Even though they were next door for only a couple of days, I've never forgotten her.

What kind of imprint are you leaving?

16

Night Life

When my parents called in the middle of the night because their furnace broke, Les went to help them. I felt a little pang of discomfort at being left alone. Well, to say I was alone isn't accurate—both our young boys were upstairs asleep. Also, our fearless cockapoo, Tuesday, was snoozing outside.

Tuesday was a lovable dog, but she had no discernment. She greeted beggar and thief, as well as doctor and chief, with sloppy enthusiasm.

She also had what I thought was a strange defect for a dog. Her barker was broken. Seldom if ever did she gr-r-r or arf. That was until . . . The Night of the Broken Furnace.

Les was gone about an hour when the barking began. I was startled at the unfamiliar sound and thought it must be a stray. I peeked out cautiously. Tuesday was on our porch, arfing in the direction of the woods.

Oh, yes, did I mention we were living on a Boy Scout reservation containing six hundred acres of woods, swamps, lakes and assorted monsters? The latter was my immediate concern.

Stop and think about it. What else would cause a bow-wow's broken barker to suddenly kick in?

Tuesday began to run from the front door, to the back door, to the front again. I knew what this meant. Whatever was out there was closing in.

I crept out of bed and began to look for a weapon. I had always believed investing in the Kirby vacuum cleaner would one day pay off. This was the day.

I took the long nozzled tube section to bed with me for protection. I placed the telephone beside me with the phone book open to emergency numbers. My heart was thumping as I strained to hear sounds of the approaching monster.

With Kirby in hand, I rotated my vision from watching the window to the door, to the window to the door, when suddenly I turned my head too far and caught my reflection in the mirror.

You want to talk about frightening . . . no . . . make that ridiculous.

I said to myself, "What's wrong with this picture?"

I've known the Lord well enough and long enough to realize He wants to be my refuge and hiding place. Here I was, trying in my anemic strength to handle this imagined invasion.

I laid down my Kirby sword and picked up the sword of the Spirit, which is the Word of God. I reviewed every peace and power promise I'd ever read. I'm not sure how long I'd been reading when fear started to drain out and quietness began to seep in, and I nodded off.

Soon I was sound asleep. I never heard my husband when he pulled up in front. I didn't hear him when he came in the door. I didn't even hear him when he entered our room. I didn't hear him until he shook my foot and asked, "What's the vacuum cleaner doing in bed with you?"

Caught with my sword down.

Are you armed or alarmed?

Feathered Friends

If anyone had told me I would become a bird-watcher, I would never have believed it . . . nor would anyone else. Did you know that the different species have unique personalities?

Ms. Hummingbird is our flitter. She has so much nervous energy her wings seem to hum her theme song, "Much to do, much to do, much to do."

She actually could conserve a lot of her strength if she didn't worry about what the other hummingbirds were doing. We have three feeders for them, but let even one of her own kind get near the feeders, and she gets herself in an uproar. Ms. Flit dive-bombs anyone who attempts to drink the sweet water, preventing others from getting the nurturing they need.

Then there's Mr. Woodpecker. What a guy—seems to always be beating his head against a dead tree. He's a handsome bird—a classy dresser with every feather in place. He taps his message repeatedly, "Picky, Picky, Picky." It seems kind of sad to see him knock himself out over the tiniest matter.

Watch out, here come the Jays. Boy, what squawkers. When they fly in, everybody knows it. A flash of blue, and then they start bossing. They think they should be in charge of the whole seed scene. The Jay family has a lot to offer, if they just weren't so pushy and demanding.

Mr. and Mrs. Cardinal are a real study. She's a dear and is content to share the feeder with all who are hungry. But that husband of hers is so brazen. Many times he won't even allow her to eat until he's done. A real chauvinist, if you ask me. They make such a good-looking couple. I just wish he were more thoughtful of her.

My friend Margret raises peacocks—beautiful but obviously arrogant birds that strut around so everyone can see their newest attire. With beaks in the air, they ruffle and fan, and if they don't get enough attention, they repeatedly cry, "Help! Help!" I guess they've done it too many times though, because no one seems to take them seriously anymore.

Let's see now, is this a list of our fowl . . . or our friends?

Oba. . .Who?

I'm not into heights, closed places, or riding in vehicles where I can't make suggestions on the maneuvering of it. Therefore, flying has never interested me—until I received an invitation I couldn't resist.

My friend Florence Littauer invited me to a leadership seminar in California. I was excited about everything except the flight. I made plans, purchased my tickets and packed my suitcase.

Flight day arrived, and my husband escorted me through the airport toward my gate. Actually, he was shoving me as my resistance grew. I remember passing a large plate glass window and seeing the ominous aircraft with a big AA tattooed on its side.

Fear can do funny things. This time, it grew feet and scampered up my arm, jumped onto my shoulder, leaned into my ear and screamed, "Run!"

My husband, using a linebacker's lunge, prevented my escape. Reluctantly, I trudged onto the plane.

My friend Rose, who was also attending the seminar, was my seat partner. That should have helped, but several minutes after we took our seats she reached into her bag and came up with a camera.

Puzzled, I asked, "Why are you taking that out now?"

"I want to capture fear in color when they start the engines," she informed me, aiming the camera in my direction.

"Oh, great, I'm shaking in my seat belt, and I've got Ms. Candid Camera sitting next to me," I fumed as the flash illuminated our row.

The day was cold, slushy and gray. I still remember the contrast as we moved up through the murky clouds and into the brilliant sunlight. As I watched out the window, there, arched in the heavens, from one cloud to another, was a rainbow.

I knew it was mine. It was a telegram from the Lord that read, "You're going to make it."

The lady beside me responded with, "Oh, look, a rainbow!"

"It's mine," I stated too abruptly. Realizing my overreaction, I softened it with, "Excuse me," and then under my breath whispered, "but it is mine." I needed that rainbow-gram too bad to share it with her.

After reaching our cruising altitude, the ride was smooth and uneventful.

Then the pilot, a man who obviously needed counseling, began to share information he should have kept to himself. "Strong Santa Ana winds are being reported ahead. We are running lower on fuel than we had anticipated. We'd like everyone to stay in their seats for the remainder of the flight."

His voice was unemotional. He didn't need to have any emotions because I had enough for both of us. I began to scan the heavens for another rainbow of promise.

Rose was reading her Bible. I think she thought it was the yellow pages as she let her fingers do the walking. She would let her Bible fall open, read a passage and then move to another.

On one portion she nudged me and said with a giggle, "Look."

I nervously glanced down and began to read. "Give that to me!" I said. "It's my other rainbow."

Listen to what it says in Obadiah (who really reads Obadiah?): "...Who says in his heart, Who can bring me down to the ground? Though you mount on high as the eagle, and though you set your nest among the stars, I will bring you down from there, says the Lord."

Thank You, Lord, and thank you, Obadiah! Now, I know Obadiah didn't pen that one with me in mind, but it sure helped this trembling traveler until we touched down.

After sharing this story at a retreat, a lady came up and said, "My version reads differently than yours. Where yours says, ' "I will bring you down," declares the Lord,' mine reads, ' "I will plummet you to the earth," saith the Lord.' "

Somehow I wasn't interested in her version. One plummet, and it would have been all over for me.

That plane flight gave me a new appreciation for terms like "landlubber," "westward ho," and "good old terra firma." Nevertheless, there is an upcoming flight I don't want to miss. I understand flight time is minimal, "...in the twinkling of an eye." We won't even have a chance to buckle our seat belt, although in-flight music will be provided—trumpets, I believe.

Yes, one glad morning with fearless abandon, I'll fly away.

Are you booked?

Messages

When our big twenty-fifth anniversary arrived, Les bought me nothing. Of course that's what I had asked for, but what does that have to do with anything? Mates are supposed to be able to decipher mixed messages. Les is supposed to discern when I mean "absolutely no" from when I mean "sort of no."

Here's the thing. Wives don't want to shoulder the responsibility of giving husbands permission to be extravagant. It frees us from guilt if we say no and our husbands don't listen to us, which of course is what we're hoping will happen. That way we can say to others, "I told him not to do this, but he did it anyway."

Les and I agreed to take a trip south as a shared gift, but I was hoping for something a little more personal. I must have been too convincing when I said, "If you get me anything I'll be mad." Maybe I should have said, "If you get me anything I might, in a minute way, be temporarily displeased."

Most of us gals secretly hope for a good "show and tell" kind of gift, especially for our twenty-fifth. It's difficult to flaunt—I mean show—a trip to your friends.

I decided to subtly retract my giftless declaration at the first appropriate moment.

A week later Les dropped me off for a speaking engagement and announced he was going to the area mall for his morning coffee. The word "mall" flashed like a neon opportunity.

With more zeal and clarity than I meant to display, I blurted out, "Why don't you buy me something!"

Oops, I probably confused him by being that . . . that . . . honest. Not that I'm not always honest . . . sort of.

When Les came back to pick me up, he had heard the message, for there, on the front seat, was a beautifully wrapped gift. I admired it for a moment and then began to remove the floral paper. Inside were layers of soft white tissue secured with a gold seal that read "lingerie."

Well, this was proof that honesty did pay; I was getting what I deserved. So what if it was a week late.

I gently pulled back the last layer of tissue and lifted out my . . . my . . . prehistoric gift. What unfolded was a long white cotton nightshirt sporting a gregarious dinosaur, which wore a lopsided hat.

This truth thing, girls, . . . you'll need to be more specific!

Pricey

I have always wanted to play an instrument. Well, not any instrument. Mostly I dreamed of playing a piano. I pictured myself moving my fingers across the ivories without looking, as I threw back my head and sang with throaty gusto. It didn't take me long to find out I couldn't sing. But piano . . . that took a little longer.

I was in my thirties when my friend Rose grew tired of hearing me whine about being deprived of piano lessons. She announced she would teach me. I was thrilled.

My husband lovingly, although somewhat reluctantly, moved an old upright into our living room. Those things weigh a ton. I could tell by the purple arteries that had inched their way out on his neck.

Not wanting his effort to be in vain, I began my serious study of the piano, certain I would soon be in concert. But I ran into an immediate problem.

It was my teacher. She quite honestly was . . . boring. This surprised me because Rose has a lot of verve. She usually was full of fun but not so as a piano instructor.

She kept insisting I do scale exercises. Either of those words I avoid regularly; combined, they were depressing. Dull, repetitious pinging sounded childish.

I explained to her that this was not what I had in mind, so she agreed to teach me some real songs.

Now, when she said real, I didn't know she was talking about "Old MacDonald Had a Farm."

How do you think it looks and sounds to have a woman in her thirties e-i-e-i-o-ing? After a few weeks of musical farming, I'd had it, and so had my family. I could tell they were stressed when the veins on their temples seemed to pulsate in time to my barnyard plunking.

"I don't want to play 'Old MacDonald.' I want to play 'How Great Thou Art,'" I stated with artistic fervor to Rose.

"You cannot play 'How Great Thou Art' until you first learn to play 'Old MacDonald,' " Rose replied through tight teeth.

"How boring, how unimaginative," I complained.

"Patsy, you don't want to learn how to play the piano. You just want to play the piano," she accused.

Boy, did she hit a chord. No way was I willing to put in the time and effort necessary to become a pianist.

I gave up my musical illusions. Les and the boys joyfully, gratefully and quickly removed the piano. Rose once again became her entertaining self.

What price is your dream?

21

Perks

Eve . . . what a perk-y lady! She definitely had advantages.

Stop and think about it. When she and Adam met, she didn't have to wonder, *Is this the right man for me?* She didn't have any immediate concerns if some sweet young thing was vying for her man's attention.

When they were wed, she didn't have to worry about forgetting someone from the invitation list or deciding who the attendants would be. No decisions were necessary on which photographer, caterer or florist. Talk about simplifying life . . .

Guess what? No mother-in-law or father-in-law conflicts. Never once did she have to hear, "Sure wish you could make applesauce like my mom." They never squabbled over whose family they would spend the holidays with.

She never had to worry about ironing Adam's dress shirts or getting the crease straight in his suit pants. There was no friction about Adam not picking up his dirty clothes, at least not in their garden home. Nor did she have to take any ribbing about where she put Adam's lost snakeskin sandals.

Eve was unique. She's the only gal who didn't have to go through puberty, peer pressure or pimples. She didn't go through the agony of handing her parents a bad report card or the knee-knocking experience of trying to explain why she was late getting home. She never once had to hear her parents say, "Why aren't you more like your sister Ethel?"

When she and Adam talked, it wasn't filled with endless tales of the good ol' days and the good ol' boys. Nor did she have to compete with the World Series or the six o'clock Eden news report.

They had a romance, marriage, honeymoon and home life that was made in paradise.

Eve had it all . . . well, almost all.

Why is it we always seem to want what we don't have?

Quiet Noise

Even when I'm still I'm not quiet. My mind is busy embroidering life, one thread at a time, according to the events of a day. Therefore, when I sit down for my quiet time, I have to battle against my mental cross-stitching.

"Sh-h-h," I tell my brain, in an attempt to focus on my prayers. I start to pray for my sons, and my mind somehow switches gears. I'm making a mental grocery list instead.

I've learned to pray with my eyes open and not to get too comfortable. Far more times than I'd like to confess, I've nodded off right in the middle of "and God bless . . ."

Now I pray wide-eyed, sitting in a straight-back chair, which has some drawbacks. I was praying for a family member the other morning when I noticed a build-up of dust under the chair in my living area.

The next thing I knew I had the vacuum out, running it around the room. Then I remembered I was supposed to be praying. I sat back down and resumed talking with the Lord.

Before long I was at the freezer taking meat out for dinner, even though I still hadn't finished my prayer time.

My mind is far too active, and my concentration span is about the length of a commercial.

I tried walking around the house and praying aloud. But then I put things in unusual places, without realizing it, keeping my family confused and frustrated.

One day I found Les looking in the refrigerator for his electric razor. When I raised my eyebrows in surprise, he simply said, "With your filing system, I just had to check."

Kneeling is a proper spiritual position, but for me it is physically defeating. I get leg cramps, go numb and limp pitifully the rest of the day. It seems like poor advertising to tell people I've been debilitated by my prayer time.

What seems to work best is writing my prayers. It helps me focus and finish before I flit off. As I write out my noisy thoughts to free my mind, it untangles the threads of my day for directed prayer. I keep my printed petitions in a notebook. I could add your name if you'd like.

Let's see now . . .
where did I put that book?

Gotcha

I loved the idea of my two-hundred-pound husband wearing short pants and a whistle. Les had taken a job as Associate Ranger for the Boy Scouts; we would be living on their six-hundred-acre reservation.

Raised as a northern woodsman, Les was more than qualified for his position. Now me, I was a city slicker. But I loved the country atmosphere.

I was determined to adapt to my new life-style. In fact, I began to daydream I would become a world-famous outdoors woman, making valuable contributions to our environment. These were rather high hopes for someone whose past experience included occasional childhood family picnics. Still, I might have fulfilled my dream except . . .

On a beautiful spring day, new life was budding all through our heavily wooded grounds. The birds were singing and so was I, as I strolled around admiring God's handiwork. The daffodils and lilacs were bursting with color and fragrance.

As I approached them, I noticed my nose was running. Within minutes I was having little fits of sneezing. Then I started itching. First my arms, next my face, then my ears. My eyes began to water and feel sandpapery.

Determined not to give in to these unpleasant reactions, I decided to get involved with a project.

I spotted a forsythia bush. Covered in brilliant yellow flowers, it was lovely except for some straggly limbs I thought should be cut off. I didn't realize there is a time to prune and a time to refrain from pruning.

As I looked for a pair of shears, I noticed my head was blocking up, and I seemed to be developing a cough, but I forged on. Finding the tools to my new trade, I began to snip and clip, feeling like quite the botanist.

I leaned down to get an unruly spray, when out of the ground came a stream of yellow jackets. They seemed to be deeply offended that I was pruning out of season and filed their grievance down my scoop-neck top.

I ran through the yard, beating on my shirt like an old Tarzan movie. My sister, who was in the yard a safe distance from me, caught a glimpse of the invasion and began to chase me.

My mom was indoors visiting with her friend Edith when she heard me yelling. She looked out the window as I ran by, quickly followed by my sister, and commented to her friend, "Oh, look, they're playing."

One good thing about living in the country is if you need to disrobe you can. So I did. The remaining attackers had to be plucked from my bod. I then took refuge in my home.

I had spots and dots, was sneezing and wheezing, itching and twitching, and I was riddled with stings. My daydream of becoming Environmentalist Extraordinaire faded with the intrusion of reality.

I had Les screen in our front porch, and that's where I enjoyed the out-of-doors.

Any intruders dive-bomb your dreams lately?

Real Estate

My mom was a mover and a shaker. She loved moving from one home to another, and it would always shake me up!

I think moving was a hobby for her. She'd buy a house, fix it up and sell it. Then she would start all over again. It always meant a different school and establishing new friendships. I made friends easily enough, but I hated leaving the old ones.

I decided when I grew up I would live in one house for the rest of my life. Then I married Leslie "The Mover" Clairmont.

Somehow my mom's mobility genes had bypassed me and entered Les. I didn't even realize that was possible.

I had felt safe marrying a man who had only lived in two homes from birth until marriage. But I counted recently, and in twenty-eight years we have moved twenty-three times.

At about house number seventeen, I decided I had moveaphobia, and I wasn't going to pack one more time.

I cried out, "Lord, it isn't fair! You know a woman gets a lot of her security and identity from where she lives."

I tried to validate my opinion with Scripture. If I could do that, I figured the next time Les made me move, I could send him on a guilt trip.

The problem was I couldn't find any Scripture that suggested we should depend on a place, position, possession or even person (other than Jesus) for our security and identity. I had to re-think my house "hold" and learn not to hang on so tightly.

I did feel encouraged when I read, "I go to prepare a place for you."

Notice place is singular. I don't have to take my Samsonite or rent one more U-Haul, y'all. I get to live in one place forever and ever. Amen.

The thought crossed my mind that when the Lord builds my husband's place, He should add on a room for my mom. Then He could put their mansion on rollers, and they could move all through eternity.

When they rolled by, I could lean out of my immovable place and wave. That would be heaven for us all!

Our home here is meant to be a haven . . .
heaven comes later.

Atmospheric Pressure

I don't feel well when I have to say "I'm sorry." I get strong, flu-like symptoms. I become nauseated. My knees get weak, my hands shake, and I get facial ticks.

If I have to say "I'm sorry and I was wrong," it's much worse. Then, along with the jerky behavior, my vision blurs, and my speech patterns slur.

I have noticed, though, that once I've said what needs to be said I make an amazing recovery.

One day Les was feeling frustrated with our eldest son over a work situation and needed to release a flurry of words. He came into my home office and spewed his displeasure about Marty onto me. Once Les said how he felt, he was ready to move past his aggravation.

After he left, I began to process their conflict and decided I could make the whole thing better. I envisioned myself as a Goodwill Angel (not to be confused with the Goodyear Blimp).

I fluttered into Marty's room and announced what he needed to do and when he needed to do it. For some reason Marty was not impressed with this angelic visitation.

In fact, he told me, "If Dad has a problem with me that's job-related, then he can talk to me."

Well, Marty might be twenty-five years old, but how dare he insinuate I was butting in? Setting aside my helping halo, in my loudest mother's voice I trumpeted my heated annoyance. I finally ended my tirade by stomping up the steps. Marty placed his exclamation point on our meeting by slamming out of the house.

I packed away my singed raiment and was still sizzling when I heard Les come in. I went down to make a pronouncement on his son's poor behavior. By the look on Les's face it was obvious he had already encountered Marty.

"If I had wanted you to go to Marty, I would have asked you," he stated through clenched teeth. "Patsy, this was none of your business."

"None of my business!" I bellowed. A cloudburst of tears followed as I ran to my room, tripping several times on my lopsided wings.

"I was only trying to help," I kept consoling myself.

When the tears and excuses stopped, I began to wonder if maybe I could have been wrong. Flu-like symptoms intensified when I realized I needed to apologize to both of them for interfering.

By the time I made my way out to Les and Marty, my vision had blurred. My head was pounding (probably from that heavy halo) as I stammered the dreaded words, "I-I was wr-wrong for interfering, I'm s-sorry, will you f-forgive me?"

Within moments we were all hugging.

As I walked back to the house, I noticed my headache and vexed vision had vanished, and it was almost . . . as if my feet weren't touching the ground.

Hey Angel Face, anyone in your sphere deserve an apology?

26

Amazing Grace

I was so familiar with our five-mile stretch of country road into town that I developed a rhythm to my driving. Sometimes my rhythm was faster than the posted pace. After following me into town on several occasions, Les mentioned I needed to lighten up on my footwork.

At times when I drove to town, I wouldn't remember the ride in because I was on autopilot. I knew every curve and turn by heart, and my mind tended to wander.

Often I would sing my way to town, and if the song happened to be a bouncy one, without realizing it, I would drive to the beat. This wasn't a problem if I was singing "How Great Thou Art." However, when I got into the rousing chorus of "I'll Fly Away," my little wagon seemed to be doing that very thing. Les warned me more than once to pay closer attention to my selections.

On one particularly beautiful autumn day, I was on my way to speak for an area women's retreat. My six-year-old, Jason, was in the back seat, looking forward to seeing his friends at the child-care room. I was into the rhythm of the road while I rehearsed my opening thoughts with great enthusiasm.

I glanced in my rearview mirror as something beckoned for my attention. There I spotted someone else who seemed to be quite enthusiastic in his desire to share some thoughts with me. A colorful character. I could tell by the red and blue circular lights on his car.

As he approached my car, I couldn't help chuckling as I pictured Les doing the "I told you so" nod.

Jason questioned, "Mom, why are you laughing?"

"Oh, honey, it's just Daddy told me this would happen one day."

The nice officer was not laughing. He leaned down and boomed with a voice that instantly reduced me to a teeny person, "And where are we going in such a hurry?"

I meekly looked into his convicting face and whispered, "Church."

"You're kidding!" he bellowed.

"I'm the speaker," I confessed. "My topic is 'Renewed Living.' I guess I'm not doing too well . . . with it," I trailed off, wishing I could disappear.

He asked me a series of intelligent questions that I could not answer with any degree of accuracy—things like "Where is your car registration?" and "Where is your title?"

I was totally in the wrong, which was obvious to all of us.

So I was amazed when he announced, "I'm going to let you go without a ticket, but you must slow down and place the proper papers in your car."

That day the officer was like Jesus. He extended mercy when I didn't deserve it.

Need another chance?

Bag It

Men and women, generally speaking, approach shopping quite differently. Men see it as a nuisance and yet a necessity. Women, however, see it as a challenge and a calling. Men tend to buy willy-nilly, while a woman investigates, evaluates and meditates her purchases . . . Unless of course it's a once in a lifetime opportunity, and she must buy immediately or lose her chance. It's amazing how many of those "once" chances a woman can find.

It drives my husband wild when I find something I like, but I take several hours looking around at other stores only to circle back and purchase that first item. Recently I resisted this urge and bought the first pair of shoes that appealed to me, only to find out later (after I wore them) that another store in the mall had them for twenty dollars less. To make matters worse, my friend had bought the same shoes—at the sale price.

This would be like a man entering a fishing contest and thinking he had won, only to have his best friend arrive with a catch twice as big and walk off with the trophy.

Sales tags are like trophies for a dedicated shopper. We would have them mounted and displayed if it weren't considered tacky. We've learned to weave our savings in our salutations.

"Nice hat; new?"

"Yes, $15.95 at Kerwin's."

"Really?"

"Yeah. Why?"

"I saw it at Lem's for $9.94."

"No!"

"Yep."

"See you."

"Bye."

You can always spot the devoted ones. They have their own language, called "Shop Talk." Words like "bargain," "grand opening," "clearance," "closeout," "refund," "coupons," "discount" and others decorate their discourse.

For me, shopping can be motivational. At times when I've felt too exhausted to clean up the kitchen, I've been able to make several loops around the two-mile mall to find the right shade of socks to go with my jeans and sweatshirt. To really raise my energy level, announce a five-minute special and watch me become almost aerobic.

Here are a couple of health warnings for shopaholics: If you browse daily, you could get Shopper's Stare from looking at one too many price tags. To prevent this, every couple hundred tags or so, take a brownie break.

Also many avid shoppers are bothered with Blue Light Bursitis from nudging their way to sales tables. They should try taking a friend and sending her through the crowd first, opening up a path.

Worst of all is the dreaded Grip. That's where the buyer and her bags have bonded, and she can't let go of her bargains. If this happens to you, train a loved one to say, "Tomorrow is another day, you can go shopping then," as they gently part you from your parcels.

Oh, yes, one more warning . . . this one from the surgeon general: "It has been proven that shopping is hazardous to your wealth."

Of course, girls, we have to take into consideration
the general who said that is a man.

Mouth Peace

I received a small catalog in the mail from an area home improvement store. I can honestly say I'm not interested in hardware, but the lettering across the front page won my attention.

In bold red print was every shopper's favorite word, "Sale." Above "sale" appeared the word "security." I need security, and I hunt for sales, so I opened their booklet to see what they had to offer.

The first page showed pictures and prices on a line of doors. The one that caught my eye was a steel door. The past week I had released several thoughts to loved ones that I should have kept to myself. If I had a steel door hinged on the side of my mouth, perhaps the next time I felt tempted to say something stinging I could slam that door shut.

The next page offered dead-bolt locks, which seemed like a good investment. Knowing myself as I do, even with the steel door closed I might kick it open to get in the last steamy word. The dead bolt could at least slow down that process.

As I scanned through the pamphlet a second time, I noticed I could purchase a door viewer for a small price. This promised to give me a 160-degree field of vision. I wonder, if I had a clearer view or a different perspective on the individual with whom I was frustrated, would I still want to sound off?

Then I came across coupons for smoke alarms. This could be the ultimate answer. If I had one installed on the roof of my mouth, when my words started heating up, the detector would go off. That would drown out all the sizzling sentences. Then, when my conversation cooled down, the siren would automatically cease and reset.

Steel doors, viewers, dead-bolt locks and smoke alarms, what a security system!

Are you wired for sound?

29

Pollution Solution

I'm told two types of people exist—those who proclaim, "Good morning, Lord," when they wake up, and those who exclaim, "Good Lord, it's morning."

Early has never been one of my day's highlights, and the morning mirror has certainly not helped to cheer me on. But I did find Scripture that helped me understand my a.m. reflection: It was "formless and void and darkness was upon the surface of the deep . . ."

I was encouraged to read that things did eventually lighten and brighten up, when God proclaimed: "Let there be light."

For me that's after I apply my blush, mascara and lipstick.

I'm married to the kind of guy who leaps out of bed in the morning, skips down the hall and sings in the shower. For years that got on my nerves.

Plus I didn't think anyone should move that quickly; he could injure something he might need in the future.

Les told people, "Patsy runs around the block every morning and then

69

kicks the block back under the bed."

I limited my exercise to jumping to conclusions, stretching the truth and dodging my reflection.

But slowly I began to realize that Les was a living example, and I would do well to learn from him. I needed a "Good morning, Lord" injection.

If this change was to take place, I'd need a plan. No, make that a miracle!

I began by memorizing, "This is the day which the Lord hath made; we will rejoice and be glad in it" (Ps. 118:24, KJV).

As soon as my brain received the jolt that a new day had begun, I would start to recite my verse—first silently, then in a whisper and finally in a shout.

My recitation started out more like a question, "This is the day . . . ?" As I continued my sunrise salute, it became a proclamation.

Gradually my new routine began to make a difference in my m.o. (morning outlook).

I honestly can't say I leap from the bed now, but I do get up. I don't skip down the hall; it's more like a crawl. I still don't sing in the shower, but I hum, and for me that's progress. No, make that a miracle!

What pollutes your sunrise salute?

Good-Bye

What do you mean join the Air Force?" I heard myself trumpeting at my firstborn son, Marty.

"Mom," he calmly responded, "when I graduate, I'm going to sign up. I might even make a career of it."

"Sure, sure, after you finish school and work for a few years then you can join, . . . say when you're forty," I suggested.

If anyone would have told me how difficult it is to release children I would not have believed it. In fact, I had observed families struggling with good-byes and thought they must be overly protective. Now that it was my turn, I was giving the word "possessive" new glue.

I tried reasoning with Marty; when that didn't work I threatened, I pleaded, I cajoled, I bribed, and then I cried. I delayed but did not divert him from finally signing Uncle Sam's dotted line.

I tried to be grown-up in my responses during our remaining weeks, but then I would see Marty, and grief would run down my face and splash off his high tops. Marty did his best to wade through my overwrought behavior. That wasn't easy because when he was home I flooded his every move with my presence, realizing he would soon be gone.

When I would pass him in the hall, I would ask him if I could hug him. He'd say, "All right, go ahead; hurry up."

I'd quickly squeeze him and then sniff off into another room.

"Patsy, when are you going to grow up?" my husband questioned in disbelief at my Velcro behavior. "Why do you think we had this boy?" Before I could respond, he would answer, "So that one day we could send him out into the grand adventure of life."

He made this announcement dry-eyed and slightly irritated with his weeping woman.

By the time the day came to say good-bye, I had released my emotions and was actually feeling pretty good about Marty's departure. In fact, I marched to the door like a brave soldier, gave him a kiss and even saluted him as he drove off.

I headed back to the house, grinning ear to ear with my new-found freedom. Then I bumped into Les, who was standing in a pool of anguish.

"Don't you have a heart?" he said haltingly. "That's our son leaving. We might . . . never see him again."

Being a woman of deep sensitivity, I realized Les had just gotten in touch with his grief, and so I tried to encourage him.

"When are you going to grow up? Why do you think we had this boy? So that one day we could send him out into the grand adventure of life," I echoed sweetly.

How many of your good-byes have brought you grief . . .
how many relief?

31

Hello

Our son Marty was about to return home from the Air Force. He had been stationed in Guam, and we hadn't seen him for eighteen months.

The night before his flight was to arrive, Les and I were at the mall, and I headed for the Party Center Store. I found cone-shaped hats with gala fringe spewing out the top, horns arrayed in sparkling glitter and multi-colored confetti shaped like stars.

This is going to be one fun reunion, I thought, as I headed for the checkout counter.

"What are you doing?" I heard a voice ask behind me. I turned; Les was standing there with his eyebrows bumping together in puzzlement.

It seemed obvious to me what I was doing, but I humored him. "I'm getting supplies for our celebration."

"Just where do you think you're going to use them?" The words sounded more like a threat than a question.

"At the airport tomorrow, of course," I responded uneasily.

"What airport?" he questioned. "Not the same airport I'm going to. If you're taking that stuff, you'll have to go to a different airport by yourself."

I couldn't believe my ears. But I decided at such a happy time we shouldn't be hassling over horns and hats, so I put the party favors back.

When we arrived at Marty's gate, two of his friends were already waiting. We sat chatting excitedly; then I mentioned that ol' Mr. Party Pooper wouldn't let me buy the delightful hats, horns and confetti.

In unison the two young men turned to my husband and said, "Thank you!"

Before I could respond, an airline representative announced the plane had touched down.

I learned that day that mothers don't need party paraphernalia to celebrate. I didn't need hats or horns because I had hands and a mouth. I started leaping in the air, trying to get a glimpse of Marty deplaning. My hands came together like clanging cymbals, over and over sounding out my joy. I began to laugh and whoop out words for the world to hear, "My son is home, my son is home!"

Then I was in his arms baptizing his uniform in a mother's relief.

At this point I'm not sure where Les and Marty's friends were . . . hmmm, now that I think about it, they seemed to have faded back in the crowd.

How about you? Do you welcome loved ones as
a loud greeter or a silent meeter?

32

Bird Brain

It started off as a Sunday afternoon stroll in the woods. I had the bright idea that Les and I should go on a bird-watching walk. Because we live on property surrounded by thousands of acres of state land, which has many miles of trails, it's the perfect setting for a leisurely outing.

First the equipment was found and organized: thirty-six ounces of diet pop, two pairs of binoculars, one bird book for ID, a pen to list all sightings and our sanguine Shih Tzu, Pumpkin.

As we headed out the door, Les asked, "Have you ever been on the trails across the road?"

By the look of the trails when we arrived, Crockett was the last one on them. The path didn't seem well defined to me, and I mentioned that to Les. He mumbled something about being a northern woodsman.

As we followed the winding path, it seemed to be closing in on us. In fact, I was thigh-high in weeds. The branches of sinister-shaped bushes and threatening trees began to smack me across the face.

"Les, get me out of here," I whined.

"You're all right. Just keep walking," he instructed, disappearing around a bend.

For a moment I was distracted from my weedy world by the sound of what I thought must be a herd of hummingbirds. It turned out to be militant mosquitoes. They motivated me to move quickly, and soon I caught up with Les. He didn't seem bothered by the mosquitoes. I think it was because of the horse flies that were devouring chunks of his hide.

My resourceful woodsman pulled off two low-hanging branches, and we took turns beating off each others' attackers.

We'd been in the woods forty minutes, and I wanted to leave—now. All I desired was to see some birds. Instead, I was branch-bruised and bug-bitten. This was no fun.

"The closest way out," Les informed me, "is the way we came in."

"No way! I'm not going back there," I stated, forging forward.

Because I had underestimated the heat, the ice cubes in the pop had long since melted. We now had Laodicean lukewarm liquid—not very refreshing but helpful when sloshed through the teeth to loosen the bugs from between our bicuspids. I learned that in certain circumstances it is appropriate for a woman to spit.

I was watching my feet as I moved through the thick undergrowth when something caught my eye. It was the rotting carcass of a mouse being eaten by gigantic black-and-yellow beetles. If I had had any lunch, I'm sure I would have lost it. I increased my pace to something close to a gallop.

We had not seen one bird. Not one!

Sweat began to drip down our branch-whipped faces, when up ahead we spotted sunlight. The woods opened up and deposited us on a dirt road at the bottom of a large hill.

As we stepped from our treacherous trail, three unsuspecting victims passed us to enter the forbidden forest. One of them had her dog on a leash. Our dog took one look at that mutt, turned around and hightailed it right back into the thickets.

Les went running after Pumpkin, making clear reference to her intelligence and her uncertain life expectancy. A short time later he came stumbling out with a repentant pooch.

Now we had to face the hill. To say we limped up it would put us in a better light than we deserve. Les had to carry Pumpkin because she was panting so hard from her run-away escapade that we were concerned she would have cardiac arrest. I was hanging on to Les's elbow for support and motivation.

Halfway up, we sat down on the edge of the road. When we started to discuss our will, I realized this had not been a positive experience for us.

Finally we stumbled into our living room. As I headed for our recliner, something caught my peripheral attention. I turned and six birds were . . . in my front yard.

Isn't that funny?
I went looking for something I already had.

Color Bind

When Les picked me up from the airport, he was dangling the house keys with obvious excitement. He had been out of work following heart surgery, and we felt grateful not only for a job but also that a house was provided for our family. He was to be the director of a Christian conference center, and we would live on the grounds.

But I had not anticipated how quickly my gratitude could seep out.

My first glance of the house left me speechless. Even the cover of night was not enough to disguise the color wheel environment of our "new" dwelling.

My friend Mary Ann summed it up when she stepped in the front door, gasped, screamed and then proclaimed, "This is ghastly!"

Truly it was. Living here would be like trying to live in a kaleidoscope that some child kept twirling. The colors collided so loudly that the place was noisy.

Come take a tour. First, picture the color orange. Got it? Now brighten it. Now intensify that. You now have my kitchen cupboards.

These reflect in interesting patterns off my luscious lime green countertops. The wallpaper in the kitchen is bursting with giant coffee pots in red, rust and orange.

The kitchen is open to the dining area, where the walls are painted powder blue. The carpeting is green and yellow shag, highlighted with oval-shaped animal stains . . . memoirs of Fido and Felix, I presume.

The dining room is also open to the living room. Both the living room and dining area have large plate glass windows with smaller windows above those. The smaller ones are painted deep royal blue with a full moon in the center of each pane (which truly is a pain). Eight full moons gave us a real orbital addition.

Someone must have read that wood adds to the decor. So, that person added a half-wall of gray barn wood, a full wall of red-stained plywood and a high but narrow wall of brown lumber.

Did I mention these walls are all in the same rooms with the moons, stains and colors? Just checking. I didn't want you to miss any of the ambience.

That evening I left there with an attitude. I didn't realize anyone had noticed until just before we moved.

Marty, our eldest, was sitting on the couch when I came downstairs. Like his mother, Marty does not care for early a.m. chatter. We don't usually get into meaningful conversations till noonish. So it was a surprise when I heard words coming from his lips.

"I can't believe it," he stated while staring at the floor.

"What can't you believe?" I inquired, amazed he was talking.

"I just can't believe it!" he repeated with greater conviction, still staring floor-ward.

This short but vague conversation was already getting on my nerves. "Why don't you tell me what you can't believe so I can't believe it with you," I insisted.

Slowly lifting and shaking his head, he gently stated, "I can't believe your attitude."

"My attitude?!" I responded defensively, elevating to my full, intimidating five-foot stature.

"Yes," he went on to clarify, "your attitude about our new home. Here you've been praying for a job for Dad and a home for our family. When it's provided, you allow something as surface as paint to distract you and rob us all of joy."

I turned and headed for the kitchen, feeling unable to defend myself. As I walked away I thought, *Who raised that kid anyway?*

I stood in the kitchen and decided I needed to talk with a woman. I prayed and immediately a name came to my mind.

"No, Lord, that's not it; try again." It didn't seem like the right name. She was a gracious and loving woman but not someone I had ever called for help. Yet the name seemed to stay pressed firmly in the forefront of my mind, so I dialed the phone.

Eleanor was home and took the time to listen to my dilemma. When I got all done with my colorful tale of woe, she simply said, "I have a poem for you."

A poem? I cried inwardly. *See, Lord, I told You she wasn't the one!*

Had she even said, "I have a can of paint for you," at least that would have been practical.

Eleanor began with her compassionate voice to quote a poem that permeated my veneer and exposed the content of my heart.

The woman who can move about a house,
Whether it be a mansion or a camp,
And deftly lay a fire and spread a cloth,
And light a lamp,
And by her loving touch give
The look of home wherever she may be . . .
Such a woman always will seem great,
And beautiful to me.

It was as if the Lord pressed that poem into my heart and did some redecorating. I hung up, knowing I had called the right person.

I pulled a chair to the middle of the room amidst the riotous color and prayed. "Lord, forgive my ungrateful heart, and help me to see what my part is in making this place into a home for my family."

As I scanned my house again, ideas began to flood my mind, and I actually got excited. First, I hired a painter.

I told him, "If you can see it, feel it or touch it, paint it. If it moves, step on it and then paint it."

I had everything painted off-white, even the wood, to give it some continuity. We scraped away our moons. Then we ripped out the stained rug and replaced it with soft gray carpeting.

Now the place looked antiseptic. Adding mauves and blues cured that. Furniture and flowers were our finishing touches.

What started off as a colorful disaster has ended up being a creative delight.

What colors your attitude?

34

Fright Flight

Yoo-hoo, Patsy," I heard someone sing out as I headed for my car in the church parking lot. I turned and saw my friend Claris waving her hand.

"Could you use some sweet corn?" she offered.

"I'd love some," I responded.

"I'll drop off a sack," she assured me as she slid into her pickup and started the engine.

I had a few errands to take care of, but when I arrived home, I was surprised to see Claris had already been there. True to her promise, I saw my bag of corn on the porch propped against the front door.

I repositioned my bag from the drugstore in one arm and embraced the corn sack with the other. I awkwardly unlocked the door and pushed it open with my knee.

Going from the bright sunlight into the dimly lit living room temporarily blinded me. I let the drugstore paraphernalia slide onto the couch, landing gently on the cushion. That freed my hands to open and examine my produce.

I balanced the bag on the back of the couch as I unrolled the top. I was still trying to make my visual adjustment from the outside, so I had to stick my head in the bag to get a corn count.

I'm not sure if my eyes focused first or my nose detected that this was not corn. What I saw were feathers, what I smelled was foul. To be more specific, it was a foul owl.

Reactions can be more rapid than reason. I simultaneously screamed and flung the odoriferous owl ceiling-ward. I went yelling out the door for my husband, who tried to assure me that the worst thing my feathered foe could do at this point was smell—no, make that stink—to high heaven, which was exactly where I had tried to throw that bird.

It turned out that some generous gentleman had found this rotting road-kill on the highway and thought we might like to stuff it for the Boy Scout Museum. At that point, I envisioned mounting the motorist, as a menace to mental health . . . mine!

Caution: Examine carefully before embracing expectations.

35

Stitches

The nine-year age span between our boys didn't keep them from big-time wrestling bouts. I pointed out to eight-year-old Jason that challenging his seventeen-year-old brother was not exactly wise. Jason seemed to have a Hulk Hogan mind-set but the body frame of Pee-wee Herman.

During a body slam attempt, he fell over a footstool and cut his head open on the corner of the wall. Les and I hustled Jason off to the emergency room, because it was obvious he would need more than a Band-Aid.

Jason was shaken and asked, "How bad is it?"

I realized that the location of his injury was to our advantage. He couldn't see it.

"Not real bad," I assured him.

"What are they going to do to me?"

Measuring my words I responded, "Fix it."

"How?"

"They're going to put it back together again," I tried.

"How?" he pushed.

I'd run out of Humpty Dumpty stalls and decided to go for the direct approach.

"They're going to stitch that thing shut, Jason," I declared.

He gasped and then groaned. "Is it going to hurt?"

"Probably," I confessed.

"But what if it hurts more than I'm able to bear?" he pleaded.

"Then you'll reach down inside of you and pull up your courage. Because you accepted Jesus as your Savior, He assures us we can do all things through Christ who strengthens us. So if it hurts more than you can bear, you pray, and He will help you."

Jason became very quiet. We pulled up to the emergency entrance, and I took him in while Les parked the car. The doctor came in, took a look at Jason's injury and began to prepare the wound for sutures. Lest things get active, he had two nurses come in, one to stand on each side of Jason.

Halfway through the process, the doctor realized both nurses were not necessary since Jason offered no resistance. Not once did Jason object to the process or cry or even ask the doctor to stop.

One of the nurses turned to leave when she noticed someone else in the room who was in need of help. I'm not sure if it was my magenta and jade skin tone or my swaying in the breeze that alerted her, but she guided me to a chair and began to fan me. Later the doctor assisted me to the car.

On the way out he said, "I cannot tell you what a privilege it was to work on a boy like that."

My husband shot me a glance as if to say, "Wish I could say the same for his mother!"

As we drove home, I asked Jason, "Did it hurt so bad you had to pray?"

"Oh, Mom, I didn't wait. As soon as you told me, I prayed," he confessed.

"What a good idea. I . . . wish . . . I . . . would . . . have . . . thought of that," I whispered.

Is your life sutured in prayer?

36

Girl Talk

You're not getting older; you're getting better!"

Who said that, and whom were they talking about? I've been looking around, and that's not what I'm seeing.

When I say "around," I mean around me. On my fortyish anatomy are ridges. I thought only potato chips were supposed to have those. These are not even rigid ridges. They're more like Jell-O. They slosh when I walk. They appear to hang in folds round about my waist.

Speaking of waste, I think it's a waste of my energy to carry these waving sacks of cellulite that are drooping off my upper arms.

No wonder women get heavier as they age—everything's turning to liquid. We are like walking washing machines. That's why we are so easily agitated and slosh a lot.

My husband and I were eating dinner the other evening when Les said, "You spilled something on your chin."

I quickly picked up my napkin and dabbed my chin.

He quipped, "No, the other one."

I don't know where those other chins came from. They weren't there when I was thirty.

I've been accused lately of looking snooty in my pictures. Don't they understand I have to hold my first chin that high to smooth out the other three?

Speaking of smooth, what has happened to my thighs? They look permanently puckered, like smocking. I feel speed-impaired at times as one leg of blubber bumps the other. Blubber-bumping can be painful.

Speaking of painful, I now get charley horses. The only place I have muscle left, and just my luck, it knots up!

One thing that has definitely increased as I age is my hair count. I have hair in places I never imagined. Like my neck. I have a three-inch follicle growing from my neck just under my third chin.

I've noticed my mental faculties are slowing down, and now I'm expected to learn a new vocabulary. Words like "menopausal"—sounds like a slow date. "Sputtering ovaries"—sounds like a rare bird or an old car. "Estrogen"—sounds like something you'd drink in outer space.

I don't know. This is all too much for me. I think I'm going to have a case of the vapors.

Gird-le up, gals. There's more to life than meets the eye.

Cookie Caper

White creamy clouds of marshmallow atop a thin layer of graham cracker, covered and sealed in a smooth two-inch tower of chocolate—the lick-your-fingers-and-catch-the-crumbs kind of cookies.

I have this "thing" for chocolate marshmallow cookies—alias pinwheels. At first I didn't realize I had a thing. I told myself I was only buying them for my family. But when I began to resent sharing those sweet treats with my husband and our boys, I took a closer look at my cookie consumption.

In a let's-get-healthy moment, I decided to give up my prized pinwheels. The problem was, one cookie was left and, well, I sort of thought it would be wasteful to throw it out.

Besides I'm not too good at this denial stuff—at least not cold cookie. But to eat the last cookie right then seemed so . . . so sudden.

Plus, when you know this is your last cookie, you don't want to just devour it. The moment should be more ceremonial. The cookie needs to be savored. It needs to be appreciated. It needs to be mine! And I knew if I did a couple of household tasks, which I should do, I wouldn't feel as bad when I ate the last cookie, which I shouldn't do.

To protect my piggish plan, I went into the kitchen and hid the cookie from my family. I tucked it in the bottom kitchen drawer behind the rolling pin, next to the measuring cups, with two hot pads carefully placed over the top to form a roof for my little sugar shack. Then I quietly slid closed the drawer and headed off to do my chores.

I cleaned my desk, dusted the living room and changed the sheets on the boys' beds. Then I headed for the kitchen, feeling I had earned this moment.

I checked over both shoulders before sliding open the drawer and removing the roof. There was the rolling pin and the measuring cups. And next to them was . . . the spot where the cookie should have been. My cookie was gone!

The next thing I remember I was running through the house, grabbing my purse and keys, and crying out, "But, Lord, I said just one more cookie!"

I sprinted to my car and hightailed it for the grocery store. I heard myself murmuring, "Just one more cookie, just one more cookie."

Finally I was in the store, moving quickly, far too quickly I realize now as I think back on the little children I had to move aside to clear the way to the cookie aisle.

At last! I had arrived and there, where they should be, were the cookies. Only one bag of pinwheels was left.

As I stood there, faced with my vice, that package packed with chocolate, I reminded myself I was an adult, and I had a choice to make. I could buy them, or I could turn and walk away a wiser woman.

Well, I ate two on the way to the checkout lane and three more on the way home.

By the time I pulled into the driveway I was full, and it wasn't just from the cookies. It was also the guilt. I was mad at myself. To think a grown woman could be controlled by a two-inch glob of chocolate!

I thought I was more mature than that. Funny, the Lord didn't seem surprised at all.

Any sugar-coated secrets in your life?

Pulling Strings

'm married to a mellow fellow. It's a good thing, because I don't think our house could take two of me. I'm so tightly strung I need the balance of someone who has his feet on the ground.

I can identify with my friend Cindy, who said her husband, Craig, is like a balloon-man. He has both feet securely planted.

She's like a hot-air balloon, flying off in different directions. Craig watches her until she gets a little too far out, and then he takes hold of the string and pulls Cindy back down to earth.

Even though I'm grateful Les is a mild-mannered man, at times I wish he would show a little more enthusiasm. Recently I purchased a new dress, and I brought it out on a hanger for Les's viewing.

"What do you think?" I prompted.

"That's nice."

"Nice?" I cried.

"Didn't you ask me what I thought of your dress?" he asked, puzzled. "Your dress is nice."

"Les, 'nice' makes me nauseous."

"What do you want from me?"

"I want dramatic; I want dynamic; I want some enthusiasm!" I demanded loudly.

"Patsy, that dress is nice," he said with quiet firmness.

So I took the "nice" dress and stomped back to the closet.

On my way across the room, Les called out, "Patsy, look! Patsy, look!"

I turned and saw my two-hundred-pound husband leaping in the air, arms stretched heavenward, exclaiming, "Wow, what a dress! Wow, what a dress!"

I burst out laughing. My steady, ground-level man was behaving like a helium balloon.

Ever notice when we try to remake a person that
we are seldom satisfied with the result?

Dynamic Duo

The flight was full. Every seat was filled with an eager traveler leaving the cold Midwest for a warmer destination.

The flight attendant handed out our lunch trays. My next-seat neighbor and I were trying to figure out our questionable cuisine (by its freeze-dried taste), when someone screamed in the back of the plane.

Ever notice when someone screams the quiet that follows seems so loud?

People react differently to a nervous moment. My seatmate began to eat faster and faster. My fork stopped in midair, and I'm sure I appeared frozen in time.

Actually, I was making some fast decisions. My first decision, because I am a great woman of faith, was "I am not going to look."

I knew if I looked I would see that the plane's back section had fallen off, and I would be sucked out. But, if I didn't look, we might land safely before I found out.

That might have worked, except the next time the girl screamed she was standing beside me. Do you know how hard it is to ignore a fellow traveler who's screaming inches from your frozen fork?

By now my seatmate had managed to place all of the food from her tray in her mouth. She had not chewed or swallowed. She looked like she had stored up enough in her cheeks for the winter.

As you might guess, the attendants busily tried to take care of the emergency. It turned out the girl was traveling with her grandmother, who had become ill, and it had frightened the young woman.

As a precaution and to make them more comfortable, they were moved to first class. Soon we noticed grandma and granddaughter were in comfortable conversation with the flight attendant. All was well.

Well, almost all. I had lost my appetite, and my seatmate was looking mumpy.

In an emergency, do you freeze, feed or face it with faith?

Weighty Matters

Scales that announce your weight? You've got to be kidding! How humiliating. I bet some ninety-pound, undernourished model came up with that winner.

The only thing worse than a robot voice announcing my tonnage is a robot with recall.

I was staying with my friends, the Hootens in El Paso, when Joyce announced, "Patsy, we have a new scale you must try."

"Oh, really," I replied with skepticism. "Why is that?"

"It's just wonderful. It talks," she joyfully reported. "It will not only tell you your weight, but it also has a memory and will tell you tomorrow if you have lost or gained."

She was thrilled. I was appalled.

I find it depressing to think that, as Righteous Robot trumpets my weight, everyone in the home hears the results. This isn't the final score for the World Series, for goodness' sakes.

"Patsy has gained five and a half pounds!" I imagined it broadcasting.

Yes, it even calls you by name.

I believe in being friendly, but calling me by my first name in the same breath as my weight is a little too intimate for me.

Next they'll put a microchip in our driver's license that heralds our age every time we pull it out of our wallets.

After a number of creative stalls, I finally responded, "No, Joyce, I'm only here for a few days. I don't think it would be productive."

Translated that means, "Ain't no way I'm leaving Texas with that information left behind."

What weighty issue tips your scale?

Buggy

I crawled into bed after midnight. Clicking off the light, I dropped my head onto the pillow. As my ears adjusted to the quietness, I began to drift off.

Then it happened. A small but definite noise. The kind of noise that causes me to become irrational and unreasonable.

I sat up in bed and shook Les.

"What's wrong?" he questioned.

"I hear a mouse."

"I don't hear anything," he stated before he even listened. He knew from experience he would get no rest if we had a mouse.

I slipped out of bed and began to move across the creaking wood floor. I stopped several times and tried to detect from which direction the chomping was coming.

This was behavior befitting a Purple Heart. In the past I would have not only insisted Les get up but also that he immediately list the house with realtors.

As I stood statue-like, I glanced down and saw something moving. No, I saw many somethings moving.

"Les, quick," I summoned.

Les jumped to his feet, motivated by the urgency in my voice. Much to our surprise, a long procession of large carpenter ants was pouring out of our heat register, doing double time across the wood floor and under the bedroom door.

We each grabbed a shoe and began to decrease their population. One of them must have yelled "run," because they scattered in all directions.

After a few moments, we stopped to listen. Once again I could hear chomping. This time the noise was very close. The sound seemed to come out of the door.

I placed my ear against the wood, and the mouse-sound magnified. Then I realized the ants weren't going under the door but inside it. The chomping wasn't a mouse, but a colony of carpenters eating their way through the door's inner layers.

Now I wanted to move!

Les, being far more reasonable, did some carpentry work himself. He retrieved some tools, took the door off the hinges and dragged it out into the night. (I was lucky he didn't drag me out.)

We were now door-less and hopefully ant-less. That night I dreamed that Les borrowed a gun and was trying to shoot the invaders out of the door.

The next morning I got up and went to my desk to work. After only a few minutes I heard a familiar sound—like chomping. I walked to my office door and realized it, too, was harboring a colony. Les then unhinged and removed that door.

Now I was coming unhinged! I was feeling antsie. I began to listen at every door, drawer and floor for the pitter-patter of little feet. I couldn't believe we could have that many unwanted guests and not know it.

Our creeping invaders were using the heat ducts as freeways. The ducts gave the critters, who traveled "antnonymously," access to every room. Since we had only seen a few here and there, we didn't realize that they had moved in their relatives. While we were sleeping, they were devouring . . . our house.

Beware of creeping little things
that splinter your house.

Airborne

Edith's combination of qualities drew me to her—her courage, creativity and confidence in God. Besides, she was fun. When I had the opportunity to be her roommate at a women's retreat, I leaped at the chance.

But when I saw the skyscraper we would be calling home, I felt "building dread." I get dizzy when I stand up straight and certainly had not planned on a high-rise experience.

Edith was delighted. For her, everything in life was a grand adventure.

As the clerk mentioned we would be on the twenty-fourth floor, I felt nauseated. Edith was elated. I hate elevators. I tried to figure out how I was going to backpack my luggage up twenty-four flights of steps.

Edith had no idea what I was going through as she headed confidently for the elevators. I had never mentioned to her that I avoided anything that elevates, levitates or regurgitates.

When the elevator arrived, a woman stepped out and proclaimed to me, "That's the fastest elevator I've ever been on!"

I immediately did not care for this woman. She obviously had not been raised properly or had chosen to ignore the commandment "Thou shalt not talk to strangers."

Edith bounded into the elevator and held the door for me. I suggested by my behavior that my suitcase had become so heavy I was unable to get to her. She stared with obvious doubt and confusion. Other people boarded the elevator and glared in my direction with growing agitation.

I knew I would have to get on or be humiliated. I sent emergency prayers heavenward, which by this time I believed to be the twenty-fifth floor.

I tugged at my luggage as I swallowed hard and reluctantly stepped on, closing my eyes so I wouldn't have to see the door seal me in.

Before I could work up a good fear, we had arrived.

Edith opened the door to our room and exclaimed with delight on finding a wall-to-wall, floor-to-ceiling window. I clung to the doorframe to keep our room from sliding off its platform.

She galloped toward the window, thrilled with the view. I began to wonder what I thought was so fun about this woman. She pressed her nose against the glass and beckoned me to join her. Then she turned, surveyed the room and suggested with enthusiasm that we take the bed closest to the window before our other roomies arrived.

"Won't that be fun," I lied.

That night I dreamed I fell off the bed and rolled out the window.

By the time the weekend was over, however, I was grateful I hadn't bolted and run but had stayed and won. I even gradually made my way to the small table next to the window and ate lunch with Edith. This was a mountaintop experience for a former agoraphobic, who couldn't wear high heels without needing oxygen.

Given a choice, I still prefer the first floor; but I've since learned being up doesn't have to be a down experience.

What has you up in the air?

Revenge

I've always been a talker, so it was natural for me, as a teenager, to take a job in telephone sales work. The goal of my position was to interest homeowners in a salesman coming by to explain our service.

Each phone girl had a script to simplify the job, to increase confidence and to keep on target. We sat in a line in front of one long desk that had partitions so we could lean forward and have some privacy when phoning. At the end of the room was a master phone where our boss could listen in on our calls.

The first week of work the boss, without warning, listened in on one of my pitiful attempts. When I hung up, he announced in front of the entire office, "Patsy, that was the worst sales presentation I have ever heard."

I was humiliated. I was infuriated. I was motivated. I attacked that phoning with fervor and determination.

At the end of the week I had more sales than anyone in the office.

By the end of the month I was the top sales girl.
And then in childish revenge . . . I quit!

How do you handle criticism?

44

Birthday Baby

When my nutritionist said, "No more sugar," I didn't have a sweet response. I did notice I was feeling better, though, when I followed her advice. But there were times . . .

We had been invited to Mary Ann and George's for a couples' Bible study. After the study we surprised our mutual friend Burt with a birthday salute. We gave him cards and sang and . . . then it happened. Mary Ann had baked a huge chocolate supreme pudding cake.

George was helping to serve, not only because he's a good host but also because Mary Ann was on crutches, recovering from an injury. Every time George entered the room with generous mounds of cake, applause and groans of gratitude filled the air.

Something began to happen inside of me as I observed this dessert distribution. It annoyed me that everyone was making such a big fuss over a sugar-infested gooey-gob of chocolate.

And why Mary Ann felt led to add super-sized scoops of vanilla ice cream was beyond me. Excessive, that's what it was.

Just look how silly they were behaving, oohing and ahing like children. It seemed to me that it wouldn't hurt a few of them to skip dessert for a while.

It was at this point that my husband was handed his mountainous masterpiece. His eyes were the size of dessert plates. He lit up with glee. Then he leaned over to me and said, "Would you mind getting me some coffee?"

"Get it yourself!" I shot back so quickly and abruptly that it surprised even me.

Les looked at me with the eyes of a rejected puppy. I felt embarrassed and ticked. I grabbed the cup and headed for the kitchen.

When I returned, Les was face first in his dish, having a lip-licking time.

I thought, *How sad that adults behave out of their addictions.*

Mary Ann called from the other room, "Patsy, could you help me?"

I walked into the kitchen, where she pointed to her dessert and sweetly asked, "Would you carry that to the living room for me?"

The injustice of it all! If you can't carry your own cake, then you shouldn't have any, is my theory.

Now, I know one should not think about tripping a person on crutches, but for one moment that thought scampered through my mind.

Grudgingly, I raced back to the main room, got rid of the calorie-crammed cake and took my seat next to Les, who now reeked of chocolate.

Then George decided to close our loving time of fellowship in prayer.

The little child inside of me throwing the temper tantrum stopped long enough to listen. As I walked out the door, I realized I was the only one with cake on my face.

Better check a mirror. I hear it's contagious!

45

Sandal Scandal

Jonah makes me giggle.

Here was a prophet waiting for orders from headquarters. When they came, he strapped on his Reebok sandals and high-tailed it out of town—in the wrong direction.

Jonah was a man who decided to live below "see" level, as he boarded the boat and went down into the hold.

I felt a little down myself when my husband came in recently from the mailbox waving a letter. I recognized the telephone company's insignia on the envelope.

"No thanks," I called sweetly. "You can take care of that."

"No," he replied, "I think you need to see this."

"It's really old news when you stop to think about it," I suggested.

"History is valuable; we can learn from it," he insisted.

I tried a spiritual approach. "Forgetting that which is behind, I press on."

By now he was dangling the expansive sheet of long-distance calls in front of my face. I felt "see" sick.

Have you ever noticed when you don't do what you know you should, you lose your vitality? Look at Jonah. After running away and going below see level, he was plum worn out. He was so tired he snored through a life-threatening storm.

My doctor used to tell me, "Patsy, you're like an ostrich. Every time life gets hard, you want to jump in bed and cover up your head."

I would think, *I must be anemic, I must be hypoglycemic, I must have PMS or TMJ or IRS or FBI.*

All I knew was I was one tired woman. Denial and disobedience are draining.

When Jonah climbed onto his ship of self-pity, he had no idea how low he could go.

I wonder if the Lord said, "Jonah needs some time by himself. Gabriel, reserve him a suite at that new Sea Sub Inn. I understand it has a lot of atmosphere."

Jonah didn't seem thrilled with his accommodations. His room didn't have much of a view, but he had plenty of running water and free transportation. The experience must have been inspiring, because he became a motivated prophet and seemed in a hurry to Reebok down to Nineveh.

All ashore that's going ashore.
Or you can stay below see level.

46

Color-Coded

oes turning forty bother you?" Les asked on my birthday.

"You've got to be kidding. Everyone has thought I was so much older for so long, it's a relief. It makes me feel legitimate," I insisted.

"You know what I hope never happens to you?" he added wistfully.

"What?"

"I hope you never get to the point, when you wave your hand to say good-bye, your underarm waves in the opposite direction."

"That quite honestly has never entered my mind," I assured him.

My husband may be prophetic, because about two weeks later, during my morning shower, every bit of tone rinsed out of my body and down the drain.

It's truly an aggravating attribute to be moving in one direction and feel your body waving in response. Stopping is the challenge, because it takes several seconds for the fleshy momentum to slow to a jiggle and finally stop. One could suffer from "whip flab" if one were not careful or stopped too quickly.

I realized Les noticed his fear had come true when Mother's Day came that year. He bought me a set of dumbbells. Actually, mine were called "smart bells." I didn't think it was a smart move on his part. I was insulted. No, make that ticked!

Finally I decided to do the scriptural thing with my heavy gift and take the writer of Hebrews' advice, "Let us lay aside every weight . . . which doth so easily beset us . . . ." I put them in storage in my bedroom closet.

I had put other things in there never to find them again. I was hoping for that kind of fate for my "bells."

Les never mentioned that I wasn't using them. I think he knew better.

Christmas came, and the memory of my Mom's Day gift had almost faded. For a moment, though, I felt some initial apprehension when he handed me a beautiful package, lest I find a tummy tuck coupon book or a fanny fixer or some other anatomy adjuster.

To my delight, however, I found a multi-colored dress with a shimmering fabric that was feminine and lovely. I was impressed. I was speaking for a luncheon in the area for a holiday celebration, and this would be perfect.

I still remember standing on a small platform speaking on "Jesus Is the Reason for the Season." To add emphasis to one of my points, I made a sweeping gesture only to notice, for the first time, the full draping sleeve.

That's when it hit me; Les had given me colorful camouflage. He had taken a more subtle approach to fleecing my flab. I laughed to myself and thought, *I'll get him later!*

What colorful cover-ups are you using?

Alert

Breakfast can be dangerous to your health. It can look innocent enough, flakes and raisins floating in milk, like the breakfast I had one morning. If I had left those raisins floating, all might have been well.

I'm not sure now if I coughed or just took a breath, but one of those rebellious raisins ran down my airpipe and wouldn't move. I hacked and coughed. I jumped up and down. Then I realized if I got real still I could breathe. My heart, which had been pounding madly, began to find its rhythm again.

I remembered a doctor was staying on the grounds (we were living at a Youth for Christ camp). If I could get to him, he would help me.

I made it to the dining hall without another fruit fit, and gratefully the doctor had just sat down to eat.

"Doctor," I whispered, "I have a raisin stuck in my windpipe. What should I do?"

He looked at me thoughtfully. After a moment of sizing up the situation, he gave his professional evaluation. "We can do a tracheotomy," he offered calmly, as he reached for his juice glass.

My heart began to palpitate wildly.

"Any other options?" I stammered.

"I could try forceps, but there's a chance the raisin would go into your lung, causing it to collapse," he concluded, as he buttered his toast.

Sweat began to appear on my deeply furrowed brow.

"Doctor, is there anything else I might do?" I whimpered weakly.

"Well," he said, hesitating while he salted his eggs, "you could try relaxing and see if it comes up on its own."

Out of all his medical insights, this one was the most appealing to me. I headed back to my apartment, wondering how that doctor could eat his breakfast while I was obviously terminating on mine.

When I got home, I positioned myself in my rocker to contemplate my fruitful dilemma. My mind began to wander to the future...

I was looking into a cemetery where two women were talking.

The one said, "What's that?" pointing to a large tombstone.

"Oh, the one shaped like a raisin?" the other responded. "I can't remember her name, but she was bumped off by her breakfast."

My heart started to jump again, and I realized I was not helping my situation with my daydreaming. I wandered into the bedroom and cautiously lowered myself onto the bed. It felt like I had a baseball in my throat. I decided to go to sleep so if it didn't work out in my favor I'd never know it.

To my amazement, I fell sound asleep. I woke up a couple of hours later—absolutely fine. I could breathe, the baseball feeling was gone, my lung had not collapsed, and I didn't need a tracheotomy. I checked all around me in bed but found no raisin. I don't know where it went; maybe it was resurrected.

All I know is I learned a good lesson—eat oatmeal.

What's difficult for you to swallow?

Scared Silly

When Carol's mom invited me to go on vacation with their family, I was thrilled. Carol was one of my best friends, and I thought a week with her would be an adventure. Carol and I were fifteen. We considered ourselves quite grown up; others seemed to find that debatable.

More than once her mom warned us that we would be staying in a ghost town. There wouldn't be much to do, and there would be no boys. We didn't care, because we enjoyed each other's company, and besides her mother could be wrong about the boys.

We arrived at the little deserted town after dark. Street lights were few and far between. Carol and I took one look at the silhouette of the tall, narrow, rickety house we were to call home that week and announced we weren't going in. It looked spooky to us, and we were scared.

The only thing more intimidating than this haunted-looking house was Carol's mom when she got angry. We had just completed a ten-hour drive, and she didn't want to argue with two sniveling teenagers regarding their accommodations.

Hanging on to each other's shirttails, we inched our way up the rotting steps into . . . a fairly pleasant home. We began to breathe easier until someone mentioned that the bathroom was in the basement.

This was not good news. Carol and I don't do basements. Who in her right mind is going to use a basement rest room in a declining house in a ghost town, especially at night? We decided then and there to exercise great restraint for the next week.

Eventually we realized the futility of that thought and had to make the downward trek. We always entered the cement and stone basement together; and while one went into the water closet, the other sat on the steps nearby.

We talked nonstop and loudly until we came back up, feeling our noise level kept us safe from the basement boogies.

One day Carol and I took a walk through the woods to Lake Superior. On such a beautiful summer day we figured we had no reason to be afraid until . . . we heard noises.

Crackling noises. Crunching sounds. Brush movement.

We glanced at each other as we remembered the stories about area bears. We turned around and began to head back to town with a quickened pace.

The suspicious sounds seemed to quicken, too.

We grabbed hands and began to run and sing loudly. Somehow we both believed that volume was a deterrent to danger. Besides, it had worked so far on the basement boogies, so maybe it would work on the backwoods bears.

We thought a popular song about Yogi Bear was appropriate for the occasion. "I'm a Yogi, I'm a Yogi Bear. Hey Boo-Boo," we sang again and again, hoping to distract and deter our assailants.

By the time we reached town, we could hardly catch our breath, our hearts were pounding wildly, and we were laughing and crying with relief.

We never did see anything . . . well, not with our eyes. But in our minds, every bush had become a bear.

What a week we had! One we would never forget. We created much of our own fun . . . and fear.

Any boogies in your basement?

P.S. She was wrong about "no boys." I'm married to him!

Misdirected

I had just disembarked from a rather bumpy flight. Les was waiting to pick me up, and I shared with him about the growing storm clouds around Chicago. He looked at me puzzled and inquired, "How would you know about the weather patterns in Chicago?"

I responded with sarcasm, "Well, isn't that where I've just been?"

"No," he stated with authority, "you've been in New York."

"I was? I thought I was in Chicago," I confessed in a somewhat lower voice.

Shaking his head in disbelief, he walked ahead of me mumbling something about not knowing how I got from one place to another without him.

Well, come on now. They are on the same side of the country. It's not like I mixed up Pittsburgh and Pasadena.

Besides, I can't help it if I came packaged with directional deficiencies. More than once Les has thought he would have to file a missing-person report on me when we have gone browsing.

The new one-stop shopping system offers, under a single roof, everything a couple could want as long as they both shall live, if they don't get hopelessly lost in the aisles in the process. With the size of today's stores, they should offer us maps, guides and skateboards as we enter.

I can't tell you how embarrassing it is to hear your name announced over the intercom. "If Mrs. Clairmont is in the store, Mr. Clairmont would like her to find her way to the front door, and he will lead her to the car."

The one-stop shop in our area is like an enclosed wilderness. I find myself wandering the aisles wondering, *What am I looking for? Why am I here? Where is my husband? How do I get out of this maze?*

Getting out of the store is just the first phase of testing your survival skills. Next is the biggie—finding your car in the parking lot. I have learned to play Car Bingo.

It works like this: Line up your vehicle with a letter on the building or an object. For instance, you might see a trash can at the end of your lane. You then count how many parking spaces between your car and the receptacle.

Let's say there are fourteen. When you come out of the store, you stand in front of the trash can. Then walk fourteen spaces . . . bingo, your car.

This is not exactly foolproof, though, because I notice that malls have a sensitivity to litter. Our mall has sixteen identical garbage bins, which if you have your calculator handy, means I could (did) look in 256 parking slots before I could shout, "Bingo!"

It's taken years, but I can sort of read a map now. If I get to you, however, don't ask me to get back to where I came from. I don't know why, but I can't reverse directions. I'm a one-way lady.

My husband believes that when I was being "knit together," somebody dropped my directional stitches.

Would you mind if I followed you . . .
that is, uh, if you know where you're going?

50

Sew Simple

A stitch in time saves nine, unless they're mine!" This quote was said by me, about me, and seconded by my high school home economics teacher.

Our class project was to make a simple straight skirt. Six weeks later, when everyone else was wearing her designer original, I was still trying to sew the darts.

My teacher was not happy. In fact, at times she didn't even look human. Her eyes seemed to glaze over and dilate when she checked my seams.

She made me tear them out so many times it was difficult to find enough solid material on which to try my next stitches.

Finally, a neighbor woman took pity on me and finished my skirt. My teacher knew an adult had sewn it, but she didn't seem to mind. In fact, she looked relieved—until she found out I had enrolled in sewing for another semester.

After announcing to the new class its sewing project, she took me aside and told me I would be doing something different. She decided I should knit a little pair of slippers. The problem was I didn't know how to knit. She assured me it would be simple.

Six weeks later I had a healthy square of knit—too large for a slipper, too small for a rug. I never did figure out how to fit it around my foot.

But my teacher didn't want it on my foot anymore. She mumbled something about putting it in a time capsule, because future generations wouldn't believe anyone could get that many stitches per square inch. I guess I held my needles a little too tight.

When I married Les, I didn't mention my home ec experiences. It didn't seem relevant—until he asked me in our first week of marriage to sew a tear in his pants' seam. I obliged, because I didn't want him to think I couldn't handle my wifely duties.

Several times he came in to see if his pants were ready. I took my time to make sure the stitches were secure.

A little while later Les came hopping out of the bathroom, unable to get his foot through the leg. It seems I stitched through one too many layers. Sometimes it's the thought that counts.

After years of Les doing our mending, the Zander family came into our lives. Margret is a seamstress, and George is a tailor.

Margret assured me that my schoolteacher was wrong, and Margret had never met anyone she couldn't teach to sew. It would be simple.

Margret began to work with me. She was patient. She was kind. She was thorough.

Then one day she looked at me and said, "Patsy, there are exceptions to every rule. From now on you bring your sewing to me."

Feeling unraveled?
There are those He sends to sew and mend.

Subpoena

O rder! Order! Order in the house!

Those words echoed in my head every time I opened a drawer, closet or cupboard. The gavel of conviction was pounding out my disorderly conduct.

I confess my house got away from me. It happened a little at a time, like mold slithering over some elderly eggplant in the back of my refrigerator. Because a person could do dust etchings on my bookshelves and grease engravings on my range, it was clear evidence was piling up against me.

I don't think all of the household disarray was my fault, though. For instance, take the socks . . . actually, you don't have to. Someone already did. Every third pair of socks, correction, that's "sock," in our home lives a solitary life.

If professionals were brought in on this case, they'd discover my dryer has a latent aggression problem. When it surfaces, the heating element disintegrates individual stockings, leaving me holding the spouseless sock. My dryer is selective and careful never to destroy two of the same kind—a true sign of a criminal mind.

I plead guilty to the webbing on my wall hangings, but I had an accomplice. My friend Norm Crane told me, "Never kill a spider. They are wonderful house guests because they are like having your own built-in silent exterminator."

Norm obviously doesn't suffer from arachnophobia.

My husband and two sons struggle with basket-phobia. They can't get close enough to my strategically placed baskets to toss in their dirty clothes. They prefer corners, chairs and doorknobs.

It does give a certain lived-in look (the kind you might find in a high school locker room after a losing game). They drape their used sweat suits and socks so that any movement of air might permeate our home with their own personal fragrance.

My junk drawer in the kitchen has overflowed, spilling shoe horns, screwdrivers, safety glasses, soda straws and squirt guns onto the countertops. This gives the room an antiquated ambience.

I'm drowning in our clutter. I think someone should provide a household suction service in which workmen could pull up in their garbage truck-type vehicle, attach a giant suction tube over the opening of the front door and then throw the switch.

The machine would create a vacuum, sucking up everything that wasn't put away. A second switch would then be activated, and the disorganized debris would be compacted into filler for highway potholes.

We would improve our environment, recycling our clutter while providing a service. Then, instead of tripping over our junk, we could drive on it.

Perhaps I could get probation if I volunteered to work on the Household Suction Service crew. We could start on my house.

Need any debris suctioned from your life?

52

Culprit

I had never kidnapped anyone before, and I was quite excited at the prospect. All the details had to be set in motion if I was to pull it off. This would require accomplices.

I called my victim's workplace, and the secretary (alias, the boss's wife) agreed to schedule a bogus meeting for the employees on Friday at noon.

Next, I lined up my mom to stay at the house with Jason while I was on the lam. I then packed a suitcase, smuggled it to the car and stashed it in the trunk.

I included only a few conspirators to help prevent a leak that would blow this whole operation. I didn't need a traitor; I had too much riding on this to let someone squeal and mess up my action.

A couple of hours away from the scene of the crime was a hotel. I called the innkeeper and told him to get things ready and to make sure I wasn't disturbed after I arrived. I promised him if he followed instructions I'd make it worth his while.

Finally the day arrived. My heart was racing with anticipation. Everything was going as planned.

I arrived at the victim's work at 12:01. Entering the front door, I asked him if I could speak to him for a moment in my car.

I had left the engine running, and when he got in and closed the door, I sped off.

At first there were verbal objections. "You can't do this! You can't do this!"

I handed him a hand-scrawled statement:

Dear Husband,
You have just been officially kidnapped. All necessary people have been notified. All business matters have been covered. Your clothes are in the trunk. Take a deep breath. Relax. I'm in charge now, and you must do as I say.
Love,
Patsy

We arrived at the Victorian bed-and-breakfast, which was decorated for the holidays. We had our picture taken in old-fashioned garb to commemorate my crime. I showered him with gifts—a shirt, pants, robe and slippers. I purchased a tape of old funny radio broadcasts. We reminisced and giggled and had a wonderful time.

I wonder if this would be considered a crime of passion? If so, I plead guilty.

Sometimes crime does pay.

53

SWAT Team

Z-Z-Z-Z-Z-ZZZZ

I had just slipped into bed when I heard the dreaded hum of a mosquito.

Z-Z-Z-Z-ZZZ

I knew it was no use trying to go to sleep until the enemy had been eliminated. I flicked on the light, which woke Les with a start.

"Whas-amatter?" he slurred.

"There's a mosquito in here . . . listen," I whispered.

Z-Z-Z-ZZZ ZZZ-Z ZZ-ZZZ

"Les, either this is the biggest mosquito God ever created, or he has friends," I speculated.

Les grabbed his discarded T-shirt to snap at the little varmints.

I spotted one and alerted Les, "There it is on the ceiling over the washstand."

At the same time, he was zeroing in on two more by the dresser. A few spectacular leaps and swats took care of our troublesome trio.

Since it was already after midnight, we were glad to turn off the light and go to sleep.

Z-Z-Z-ZZZZ

"You're kidding," Les growled.

I reached over to my nightstand, running my hand down the cord to the switch and once again illuminated the battlefield.

It was us against them, and they had come armed for battle. Their entire platoon had been called in. They attempted several strategies— the old dive-bomb-the-head maneuver and the tricky blend-in-with-the-wood-and-wallpaper routine.

Les outdid himself with breathtaking counterattacks. I think the most impressive ones were as he bounced up and down off our mattress and in one swipe wiped out two of those little scoundrels. Of course, his shocking-pink, striped boxer shorts definitely added flashes of color as he leaped back and forth about our boudoir.

I acted strictly as a spotter, carefully camouflaged under the sheet, lest I become their next juicy victim. Some of their kamikaze pilots had come in and were doing suicidal spirals at our anatomies.

But no fear...Les was here! My husband was taking his call to active duty like a real soldier, with true dedication. He was now a two-fisted fighter, T-shirt in one hand, fly swatter in the other.

I became a little nervous, though, when he leaped over me in attempts to get escaping prisoners.

About 2:00 A.M. my dedication faded, and I fell sound asleep. I woke at 8:00 A.M. to find my husband standing over his trophies.

He had killed more than forty mosquitoes before he discovered and closed off their access point. He had twenty-three bodies lined up for all to see. The rest were splattered in various spots in our bedroom. Unlike me, who had gone AWOL, he had stayed faithful until the war was won.

Are you steadfast in life's battles?

Sow's Ear

The flight attendant struggled to position my purse under the seat, insisting it must be stored before takeoff lest it "get loose" and endanger fellow passengers. I noticed a smirk at the corners of her mouth as she said, "I bet you can hold a lot in there."

I'm sure it must look comical to see a five-foot lady carrying a six-foot purse, but I find it a necessity. I remember a fellow passenger once commenting as I struggled to the ticket counter, "Lady, it's hard to tell if you're carrying that purse or it's walking you."

Men don't understand; women have stuff. Important stuff. One never knows what one may need when one leaves home.

In my purse I carry practical provisions, like a pencil sharpener, nail polish remover, vitamins, flashlight, collapsible scissors and drinking cup, five tubes of lipstick, tweezers, floss and other stuff too numerous to mention and too valuable to leave at home.

My purse is an extension of my home. I have every room represented in the folds of my handbag.

I tried a few smaller purses, but I had to carry two, and even then the tops wouldn't close.

My friend Emilie recommends you carry little purses inside your bigger purse to keep the contents organized. I tried that, but I needed so many little ones, it made my paunchy purse look like it had a fertility problem.

Some purses are designed with compartments. I owned one with so many built-in pouches and pockets that I needed a directory to remember where I had stored my stuff.

Today's fad is belly bags that tie around your waist, leaving your hands free. Great concept... for those who have a waist. There's no way I'm going to add inches to the bag already permanently affixed to my bod.

Businessmen understand purses better than they let on. Take note of their briefpurses—excuse me, briefcases. That's where they carry their stuff. Pens, paper, passport, paper clips and paraphernalia.

I was almost cured of my handbag hang-up when I was diagnosed with purse-itus. That's when your purse straps embed themselves in your shoulder, leaving you bound to your belongings.

After a temporary separation, my bag and I have been reunited and are working out a contents settlement. I've agreed to lighten its load; and in return, my purse has promised not to be such a weight around my neck.

What kind of "stuff" are you carrying?

Vantage Point

Winter ... brrrr ... I never liked the cold.

For years I whined my way through winter, feeling justified as I listened to many others complain about the cold. Then we moved to a Boy Scout reservation on six hundred twenty-five acres, and I realized it could be a long, lonely winter if I didn't find some way to use my time. I decided to take up cross-country skiing.

First, I had to purchase my equipment. That was fun. I chose adorable powder blue ski pants, matching jacket, a sweet little knit hat, fluffy mittens, groovy goggles, floral long johns, cute color-coordinated shoes, darling little poles and oh, yes, some skis.

Les did not think it was wise for a non-athletic novice to go sliding off by herself into half a mile of heavily wooded acreage. I kept assuring him I could handle this.

I can still hear him calling to me as I glided out of sight, "If you get lost out there, I'm not looking for you till spring."

There's something about having the right equipment that can give one unrealistic confidence. I felt as though I looked professional—besides, how hard could it be to walk in the snow?

I was amazed how quickly I picked up a rhythm. The snow must have been just right for gliding, because I was moving well, and my overrated view of my ability was growing with every stride.

At this point I passed the hill . . . a sizable hill . . . a steep hill. It seemed to be beckoning me, tempting me, daring me. What could there be to tucking my poles and bending my knees? Life was meant to be lived. I decided to go for it.

I positioned myself confidently and then leaned forward. Who would think one little lean could start one in such a downward direction? The wind blowing briskly about my face reminded me of the exhilarating challenge of life. I believe it was at this moment that I spotted the lake, which reminded me of the excruciating pain of death.

I seemed to be headed for the thinly ice-covered water at an increased rate of speed. I meant to learn how to swim, I really did. (This thought seemed a little hindsight-y.)

Being perceptive, it didn't take me long to tune into one fact—whoever designed these skis forgot an important feature: the brakes. You would think that a backup parachute would be required at the time of purchase. Where's Ralph Nader when you need him?

No fear though, for there, before my eyes, was an escape route—a grove of fir trees. Actually, I could see now that I couldn't miss those babies if I wanted to.

Leaping sideways to try to slow my momentum, I bounced off almost every tree trunk in the woods. Limbs met my face and body with a whipping force.

Finally I came to a stop. Wrapped securely in bark at the base of a tree, I lay very still. Snow is not as soft as it looks.

Slowly I tried moving body parts that just minutes before were gliding merrily along with little effort. Now some parts had no feeling while others had a great rush of pain.

Les's face flashed through my mind. I could almost see that "I warned you" look, followed by a smirky smile. I determined then to keep this story under my skis.

Discomfort began to attack all parts of my body. Nothing seemed to be broken, just painfully re-arranged.

The hill had acquired mountain proportions. I was scaling it on my knees while dragging my slightly abused ski equipment behind me. I had the suspicion that someone was videotaping this escapade, and the next time Les was watching sports, I would be featured in the "thrill of victory and the agony of defeat" segment.

I buried the bent equipment in the snow beside the house and slipped onto the porch. Swallowing my groans, I made my way through the house to my room, sat down on the bed and started the uncomfortable task of disrobing.

Just then Les walked in.

I'm not sure if it was my lopsided groovy goggles, the pine cones hanging off my sweet little hat, or the evergreen needles protruding from my front teeth, but he sensed things had not gone well.

He was actually quite merciful. He only sang thirty-two rounds of "The Old Gray Mare."

When he left the room I looked down and saw the packaging my goggles had come in. It read, "High-altitude glasses." I thought, *That's what I need*. Not ski equipment but the advantage of a Higher perspective. Perhaps then I would have chosen tatting for my winter sport.

What was that again, the thing that goes before a fall?

Weather Watch

My friend Don Garrett tells me I talk twenty-five miles per hour with gusts up to fifty. My husband says that is ridiculous—my gusts are at least a hundred.

Gusty people are easy to identify. We are the ones broadcasting our biographies to the world. Our friends run from us in the grocery store. We are part of the reason Reeboks are so popular. People spot us by the cereal and quickly jog three aisles over to the dog food just to avoid us. They give up their Wheaties for Woof Woofs and figure it's a small price to pay.

Usually friends feel guilty playing dodge-'em cart, but they know if they ask how we are, we'll start at birth. Most people don't have that kind of time, interest or attention span.

When two Gusties meet up, sprint for cover. Even a windbreaker won't protect you from their gale-force exchange.

They start talking before the grocery baskets stop rolling as each attempts to get his or her news out first. This is an important part of the strategy, so that at the end of the first speaker's whirlwind of words, that person can announce, "Have to run!" The plan is to escape the blast of babble from the opponent.

Gusties have incredible lung capacities. They know if they take a breath, someone else might get control of the conversation. They speed-speak, which requires them to mentally remove all punctuation, enunciation and hesitation.

When two prolific Gusties visit, they often speak in overlap. That's where before one can finish a thought, the other speaks over the top of the victim's words and runs away with the spotlight. The main objective is not what is being said but who gets to say it.

Receiving a telephone call from a Gusty can leave you feeling blown away by the velocity of verbosity. It's amazing that a person can utter so many words and actually say so little.

The good news about Gusty callers is that you can lay down the receiver, complete several tasks and pick up the phone without having them miss you. They are what you might call self-contained conversationalists.

If you meet a Gusty with PMS or one in mid-life, watch out! It adds a whole new meaning to "the winds of adversity." Meeting one is like trying to hug a hurricane. Storm warnings should be posted during these seasons for the safety of the public.

Do you leave people with a wind-blown look?

Visitors

Les and I have been married . . . forever. Our marriage didn't start in paradise but in a basement. It didn't start out like Eden but more like eek!

Our first apartment was in a monstrous, ancient, decrepit, mansion-type house. Ours were the only basement quarters. That should have made us cautious, but we were young, inexperienced and poor. We had to live in the inner city to be close to the bus station so Les could get back and forth to the military base.

After we paid the rent, we had five dollars for groceries and bus fare. We bought milk, bread and bologna. That simplified meal planning.

Les spent every other night at the barracks, which meant I was alone. This was a new experience for me.

Our apartment was furnished in early ark artifacts. We had three rooms and a bath. Because the rooms were lined up on one wall of the basement, the floor plan was like a conveyor belt. We had to go through the living room to get to the bedroom, and through the bedroom to get to the kitchen, and through the kitchen to enter the bathroom.

Our bathroom was unique in that you had to stand in the doorway to take your shower. It seemed the shower head was permanently jammed in a northeast direction.

One night when I was alone and bored, I decided to eat something. I thought my big menu decision was whether to have my bologna sandwich with or without a glass of milk. I was wrong.

When I opened the cabinet that housed my bread, I found other tenants. Roaches. Hundreds of roaches. The bread bag hadn't been retied securely, and it was alive with these pilfering pests. They were feasting on my valuable staple.

I was repulsed and angry. Slamming the cupboard shut, I flicked off the light and fumed back to the living room.

As my hunger increased, I reasoned that those nasty varmints couldn't get into the refrigerator where the milk and meat were safely stored. So I went back to the kitchen.

As I turned toward the refrigerator, I saw something move. I froze in my tracks and so did it. I was about three feet from the biggest rat I had ever seen. Well, actually it was the only rat I had ever seen.

In slow motion I climbed onto the tabletop as a scream moved through my body and out my lips. My new roommate decided to vacate by scrunching under the kitchen door. This door led to the rest of the basement, which was a dark maze filled with furnaces for the upstairs apartments.

While perched on my platform I cried . . . profusely! I didn't know anyone, we had no phone and no money, it was late, and Les wouldn't be home until the following day. We didn't even have a TV or radio that I could turn on to scare the rat and give me a diversion.

When I ran out of alternatives, I remembered the Lord. It had been a while since I had talked with Him, but I wanted to now.

After an emergency prayer time, I cautiously made my way off the table. Then I quickly turned on every light in the apartment. I stuffed towels in the scrunch space under the door. Then I sat in the living room and plea-bargained with the Lord.

Eventually, I braved my way to bed, praying all the way. As I lay back against my pillow, an incredible peace came over me. I felt so safe and cared for. I could feel the stress of my trauma ease out, and I felt myself falling asleep.

Have you noticed when you run out of places to turn,
He's always there?

58

What a Pain

Before I even opened my eyes, I knew I was in trouble. My stomach felt as though it was an automatic butter churn. The paddles were doing double time, and everything in there was clabbered. My head felt light, and when I opened my eyes, my body seemed to jounce.

I sat up abruptly, hoping to recall my head from the ceiling. It didn't work.

I carefully inched my way to the edge of the bed and tried to figure out what was going on. My twirling head made it difficult to reason.

I thought maybe I'd feel better if I got up and moved around. I slid off the side of the bed onto legs like Jell-O and hugged the wall. I decided I was dying.

"Les, Les," I groaned pitifully down the stairs.

"What?" he called back cheerfully from his office.

"I'm sick. I think I'm dying," I whimpered, resenting his good mood. I'm into group suffering. If I'm not doing well, it's not that I want you to be sick exactly . . . miserable will do.

Les bounded up the steps and then walked too heavily down the hall, hurting my now throbbing head. He took one look at me embracing the wallboard and announced, "You look like you're dying."

I didn't have time to thank him for his words of encouragement, because I had a physically compelling desire to visit, if not move into, our bathroom.

I have always found kneeling in front of a ceramic centerpiece humbling.

Finally I moaned my way back to my bed where I found Les trying to stifle a case of the giggles under his pillow.

"I'm sorry," he confessed, "but if you could only hear yourself."

I personally find it helpful to moan if I am in pain. The more pain, the louder I moan. Besides helping me deal with my discomfort, it alerts everyone within a one-mile vicinity that I am not doing well. I am certainly not opposed to get-well gifts.

I reminded Les of that and told him he had better hurry because I wasn't sure how long I could hang on.

Turns out that my terminal illness was a short-term flu. Just about the time I thought I was taking my last breath . . . I was well.

Can you handle pain, or. . . are . . . you one?

59

Wild Bunch

I'm staying on beautiful grounds that belong to my friend Verna. While I'm resting and writing, I'm in a home tucked in the woods. God's fingerprints are all around . . . as well as His sense of humor.

I was reading one morning when I heard what at first sounded like a squeaky wheel. As the sound moved closer, I went to the window.

Much to my surprise and delight I saw a flock of wild turkeys. Counting heads was hard because they were moving so quickly, but I figured there were at least forty of them.

They appeared to be having an intense meeting. Having divided into opposing sides, they were in a heated debate. One group would aggressively storm their opponents, gobbling forcefully. The others would then respond confrontationally, their gobbles sounding at times more like screeching. It seemed as though those yelling loudest were the most intimidating.

One small group separated from the others in pursuit of a lone turkey, apparently trying to whip him into shape or get him to submit. They surrounded him, backed him into several trees and didn't let up until he hightailed it to the back of the pack.

Then one of them spread his masterful tail feathers and began to strut. Immediately the flock settled down and followed the flamboyant one single file into the woods.

As I observed these turkeys, I couldn't decide if I had just witnessed a political rally or a church board meeting.

Gobble Gobble

Bus Stop

Jason, our youngest, has two goals in life. One is to have fun, and the other is to rest. He does both quite well. So I shouldn't have been surprised by what happened when I sent him to school one fall day.

As Jason headed off for the bus, I immediately busied myself, preparing for a full day. The knock on the door was a surprise and disruptive to my morning rhythm, which is not something I have a lot of. I flew to the door, jerked it open, only to find myself looking at Jason.

"What are you doing here?" I demanded.

"I've quit school," he boldly announced.

"Quit school?" I repeated in disbelief and at a decibel too high for human ears.

Swallowing once, I tried to remember some motherly psychology. But all that came to my mind was "A stitch in time saves nine" and "Starve a fever, feed a cold," or something like that. Somehow they didn't seem to apply to a six-year-old drop-out dilemma.

So I questioned, "Why have you quit school?"

Without hesitation he proclaimed, "It's too long, it's too hard, and it's too boring!"

"Jason," I instantly retorted, "you have just described life. Get on the bus!"

Well, I cannot tell you how many times the Lord has had to echo that counsel back to me—times when I've questioned, "Lord, You say You'll never give us more than we can bear. You must not be looking. This is hard, very hard!

"By the way, Lord, it's been lasting a l-o-n-g time. And truthfully, it's getting bo-ring!"

About that time, in the recesses of my mind, I hear the refrain, "It's life; get on the bus!"

Bus token, anyone?

61

Prophet Profile

G od purchased His people to plant them in the place of His prosperity. Let's peer into the power-packed pages of our Protector's priceless promises to see this very thing.

In His publication, on the first page of Exodus, we see God's people pleading in prayer, as prisoners of pharaoh because of population problems. When God's people pray, He delights in providing.

But point two becomes perplexing when the provision for His people is put in a pond, pulled from the basket and placed in pharaoh's daughter's arms. She beats a pathway back to the palace to prepare him to become a prince.

Problems arise for Moses when he becomes a perpetrator. The palace becomes a perilous place, so he heads for the pasture.

Now how could pasturing stupid sheep ever prepare you to lead God's people? Perfectly!

We begin to see the process to become one of God's VIP's ... plagues, Passover, pillars and piled-up water that became a pathway for some and a precarious place for others.

Perhaps you've been pondering your future plans and feel perplexed. Well p'shaw y'all! Just remember Moses, who went from the pond, to the palace, to the pasture, to the pinnacle, to view the promised land before entering paradise. Praise the Lord.